Todd Holton

How a Praying Global Village Brought Back the Dead

With
Megan S. Holton
&
Daniel V. Runyon

Todd Holton: How a Praying Global Village Brought Back the Dead
With Megan S. Holton & Daniel V. Runyon

Editorial Note: Multiple versions of the Bible are briefly quoted, some that capitalize pronouns referring to God and some that do not.

Cover painting by Bethany Posa
Back cover and some interior photos by Kerri Conrad

Publisher: Daniel V. Runyon
Spring Arbor, Michigan 49283

Print price: $15.00
eBook $7.50
Print ISBN: 978-1530908769

Find eBook and print formats of this book online.
Search: *Amazon.com: Daniel V. Runyon: Books.*

Dedication

To the next generation of Holtons and their descendants as a story of encouragement to tell others of the love of Christ and the power of prayer. To God be the glory.

About the Cover

And he carried me away in the Spirit to a mountain great and high, and showed me the Holy City, Jerusalem, coming down out of heaven from God. It shone with the glory of God, and its brilliance was like that of a very precious jewel, like a jasper, clear as crystal. It had a great, high wall with twelve gates, and with twelve angels at the gates. On the gates were written the names of the twelve tribes of Israel. There were three gates on the east, three on the north, three on the south and three on the west. The wall of the city had twelve foundations, and on them were the names of the twelve apostles of the Lamb.
—Revelation 21:10-14

Contents

Introduction

Todd Holton died very early on Sunday, May 31, 2015, of cardiac arrest—but no coroner was there to pronounce him dead. Instead, his son Philip was there, and he knew a thing or two about CPR. He performed it relentlessly until early responders found their way to the old farm house just south across the river. They used the defibrillator three times to get his heart beating again and then transported him to Allegiance Hospital in Jackson, Michigan.

Knowing that a brain without oxygen can die within six minutes, the medical team placed Todd's body in an ice bath that lowered his temperature to 91.6 degrees in an effort to preserve organs and brain function.

Medically speaking, a person with a restored heartbeat is "back from the dead." In Todd's case there was great uncertainty because of the amount of time his brain and other organs were without oxygen.

Todd's daughter-in-law, Meg Holton, kept a journal of much that happened over a period of ten days to reunite his mind and body as a self-aware human being. The notes she posted for relatives and friends—including missionaries and believers from around the world—on the *CaringBridge* website, document what happened to Todd's body while physically in the "deep freezer" and mentally in a coma. She also recorded the prayer requests and their answers as the global church bathed these life-preserving efforts in prayer.

Medical science thoroughly documented everything done biologically during Todd's recovery. Other events also took place—things only Todd can vouch for—that no science can explain. These events included encounters with fascinating people long dead, and intriguing visions of heaven.

Todd met and conversed with his beloved Grandpa Linford Kingsbury, enjoyed the piano artistry of deceased musician David Rupert, and saw colors that can't be painted—white on white on white. Look through Todd's glimpse behind the veil of death to experience the mighty hand of God at work through his praying global village.

At the time of his death, Todd was 54 years old with a two-year agricultural degree, a farm, a job at Spring Arbor Lumber, and a family and church that refused to stop loving him. By no coincidence, his wife's name is Faith.

This glimpse into Todd's folksy Americana lifestyle in rural Michigan will delight even those who doubt the authenticity of his testimony or the fellowship of the saints in his world.

Chapter 1

A Normal Spring Weekend

Late on Friday after work at Spring Arbor Lumber, I got home to discover Allegra (Stoetzel) Butler was back from Alaska and visiting my house— she wanted to bring two sons of a friend out to fish for bass and bluegill in my pond. But the kids were more interested in chasing Dale Thorne's sheep. I was letting him pasture them there to keep the grass mowed around the pond.

I was perturbed about the kids chasing the sheep because I used to have Angora goats, and if you chased them too much, the animals get really hot and could die. So I scolded them: "Would you like to be chased while wearing a heavy wool coat in warm weather?" Allegra said that was the first time she ever saw me so upset.

The next morning, Saturday, May 30, 2015, I went to the Spring Arbor Café at 6:45 a.m. to have breakfast with a group of mainly church people who were part of the Tuesday golf group (although I don't golf). We've been meeting for a couple of years.

Usually, there are ten or twelve of us and we just hang out and talk about everything: politics, church, Gospel Barn stuff, farming, the lumber yard—anything that strikes our fancy. I feel like a spring chicken in that group because at age 54 I'm one of the youngest people there.

For breakfast I generally have a "Todd in the hole"—some call it a "Toad"—it's a big pancake with a hole in the middle filled with an egg over-easy, and then strawberries and whipped cream. And usually I have some bacon. I don't particularly like coffee, but I drink it there.

On Saturday we open the lumber yard at 8:00 and were pretty busy that morning. I remember taking a delivery of lumber and trim work to a builder—Jason Swihart—to a site on South Jackson Road where he was remodeling a fire job—he was saving a house that had burned.

We close at noon on Saturday, and Kevin Ganton had called wondering if I wanted to go with him and Mike Ykimoff to Cabela's in Dundee. I said, "Sure, I have a little time." Cabela's sells ear protection and sound equipment for hunters. Kevin is pretty deaf—we always kid him about it—so on that trip we talked him into having a free hearing test at Cabela's. He failed miserably and we've teased him about that ever since, but he still won't get a hearing aid.

Up in the balcony restaurant overlooking a huge, man-made mountain populated with all kinds of taxidermied wildlife, we ate moose and elk burgers. Then I went home and did chores. When Faith asked if there was anything we'd like to do, we decided to watch our DVD of *Sherlock Holmes 2* and then headed for bed. Our four-year-old grandson Palmer lives with us, but he was away that weekend so we didn't have to put him to bed.

I said it was a typical spring weekend, and I guess it was because I'm always doing something I love on a weekend. But really, there's no such thing as typical on my farm. The weekend before, I might have been out planting corn or soy beans on my 240 acres. I already had 120 acres of wheat in the ground.

Sometimes when I'm not pressed for time on a weekend, I like to work on one of my old cars out in the barn. I'd been doing some wheel work on my 1913 Jackson: repainting some nuts, bolts, and lock rings. I had bought new tires and had found some missing parts through Dean Nelson from Minneapolis, Minnesota, who found the parts at the

Bakersfield Car Show in California. I had those parts on a wire and was spray painting them.

Other things I might have been doing on a Saturday include working in the yard, socializing with someone, cutting firewood, or looking after the chickens. There's always something to do.

Usually I get to bed between 10 or 11:00 p.m., but that night, thanks to watching the movie, it was close to midnight. The majority of the time Faith and I don't go to bed at the same time because Palmer likes to have someone sleep in the same room after he has been tucked in. When I put him to bed, we tell stories—he likes me to tell him Chubby stories or Inky and Dinky stories.

His favorite story is the one where Chubby rides the school bus and gets his cheeks stuck in the door and asks the bus driver to please open the doors. I push my cheeks together to show the doors squeezing my cheeks together, and Palmer laughs.

If Faith tucks him in, then I'm probably watching the news on channel 47. We just have rabbit ears so we can get about five stations. If I'm not watching the news, I might be reading. At that time I was actually reading the early American evangelist Redfield's book *Live While You Preach*. "As long as you preach, you can live," God told him, so he kept on preaching as long as possible.

So Faith and I were going to bed, and she asked me about my day at work. I mentioned the story of Rex Cooper, one of my drivers at the Lumber yard whose daughter had been in a car accident and had totaled her car. Thankfully, she escaped with just a few minor injuries.

We were talking with the lights out just after I was telling her that story, and that's when she heard me gasp for air and take a big breath. She thought I had fallen asleep and had started snoring, but when she heard me gasp the second time, she thought, "that doesn't sound right," and she flipped on the light.

I gasped a third time, and that's when she saw my eyes roll back into my head and realized I had stopped breathing. She yelled down to our son Philip (Palmer's dad) through the cast iron floor register that opens into the living room: "Phil! Grab the cell phone! Call 911! Dad's not breathing! And get up here!"

Philip works at the Jackson County Youth Detention Center where he was trained in CPR. He started the CPR by doing 30 chest pumps and then blowing in two breaths. He did that for a long time.

Faith said it seemed like forever, but it was probably about 12 minutes before EMTs arrived and brought their equipment upstairs.

That was early on a Sunday morning, and I don't remember anything until a week-and-a-half later on Wednesday afternoon when I woke up. I'm told they had me doped up on one of the same medications that may have killed Michael Jackson.

Within a few hours of my admission to the hospital, Faith and I had many visitors. Our son Phil, my parents Roy and Joan Holton, my brother Kyle, our son Nathan and his wife Meg, and friends Kevin Ganton, Mike Ykimoff, Darold and Marg Hill, and Pastor Mark VanValin—all of these came to see me before the Sunday service! The picture below is of Darold Hill (left) and my dad (right) praying for me.

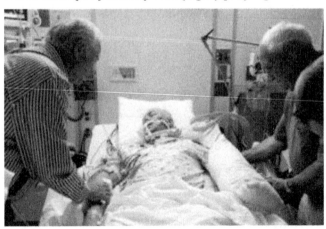

Chapter 2
Cardiac Arrest

My daughter-in-law, Meg Holton (reading to me in the picture), kept an account of the medical protocols and procedures carried out on my behalf. She wrote daily posts on the *CaringBridge* website for our many relatives and friends—including missionaries and nationals from around the world. A lot happened when I was in a coma. Of course, I remember none of it, so I'm very grateful to her for what she wrote.

CaringBridge Update—June 1, 2015 10:27 a.m.

Early yesterday my father-in-law (Nate's Dad) Todd Holton suffered cardiac arrest. He was brought to Allegiance Health Hospital in Jackson on the

midnight hour. He has undergone several tests: blood labs, EKGs, chest X-rays, CT scans, and others. After a heart catheterization, Todd's cardiologist found that he has cardiomyopathy. He is sedated and now being put through an arctic sun treatment/hypothermic process.

Our prayer request and hope is that Todd suffered only minimal neurological damage. When someone's heart stops and they are without oxygen for any significant length of time, it affects the brain and heart.

This is a critical time of waiting. We pray that the Lord's hand will be evident and at work in the next 48-72 hours. May God's hands touch him in such a way that his recovery is even better than "best case" possible. After this period we will know much more about his neurological function. Then we will be able to move forward with cardiologic care.

Please pray with us. Let's come together before our loving, caring God, and intercede for Toddy! Our God fights for us, and Todd is a fighter, too!

Psalm 24:10: *Who is he, this King of glory? The LORD Almighty—he is the King of glory.*

— June 1, 2015 10:30 a.m.

Todd has been doing well. He is part way through his arctic sun treatment. He has 24 hours of the "maintenance stage" which he will conclude this evening. At 5:00 p.m. he will start the rewarming stage of arctic sun. This will be a critical time for him as it will be a big shift from cool to warm. This rewarming stage will take twelve hours, and then the neurologist will start to look at eliminating sedatives.

The neurologist will go from there. Depending on how things come along, he will do some simple tests to evaluate Todd's neurological function. This will tell us a lot about where Todd stands. We are calling on God to give us a better-than-best-case scenario. Todd is doing as well as possible right now. Our nurse last night (Mary, we love her), was very optimistic about Todd's progress. *Praise God from whom all blessings flow.*

Prayer requests: The switch from maintenance stage to rewarming stage will take place tonight. This is a time when a "shift in fluids" occurs and we are praying that the transition is smooth.

Also, please pray about tomorrow morning when the doctors and nurses will consider taking Todd off of sedation. We are praying that the arctic sun treatment and God Almighty have preserved his energy, organs, and—most importantly— his brain.

We cannot express our great, great thankfulness to the Lord for His mighty power and deep love throughout all of this. He has answered so many of our prayers, and it is evident that His hand was in this, even before it all started. He has been so good to Todd and so good to us.

Lastly, we thank you all. Prayer chains have been formed around the planet, interceding for Todd and the medical team and our family. We have felt an overwhelming amount of support, love, and encouragement. We are astounded by you amazing people. Thank you to the hundreds of people who have checked in with us, prayed with us and for us, visited us, and helped us.

Although Todd is doing as well as he can, we are still at a critical time. We cannot get up off of our knees. Now is a waiting time, but more importantly, a praying time.

Psalm 40:5: *Many, LORD my God, are the wonders you have done, the things you planned for us. None can compare with you; were I to speak and tell of your deeds, they would be too many to declare.*
Praise God from whom all blessings flow.

—Day 2, Update 2 - June 1, 11:11 p.m.

The rewarming process started tonight at 5:30 p.m. and will end around 9:30 a.m. tomorrow. The switch from cool to warm has so far gone quite well. The nurses are keeping close watch over his lab results every couple of hours and thus far they have come back normal.

One of the most important things during this time is his electrolyte levels as the change from cool to warm causes a shift in his fluids. Also, sedative weaning will start tomorrow morning before the rewarming process is completed.

While tomorrow may bring more information regarding Todd's neurological function, we still may not know much before the next few days. Todd is doing as well as can be expected for now. What a trooper!

A specific prayer request is for Todd's electrolytes during this change. Also, we are praying that the transition off of sedation is a smooth one. Lastly, pray that the Lord will intervene in a powerful way resulting in a better-than-best-case scenario.

God's gracious and powerful presence is overwhelmingly evident. The family has felt the many prayers, the outpouring of love and encouragement, and the support of everyone through visits, texts, flowers, food, and emails. We are grateful to God for his goodness, to you all for your love, and to the medical team for their great care. We will send out another update tomorrow. Also remember to pass along Todd's site at CaringBridge.org to anyone who is not on Facebook.

Psalm 27:13-14: *I remain confident of this: I will see the goodness of the LORD in the land of the living. Wait for the LORD; be strong and take heart and wait for the LORD.*

—Day 3, Update 1 - June 2, a.m.

This morning brings good news in that Todd's night was uneventful. All of his labs have been coming back very good and he is doing well. Praise God! Rewarming will soon come to a close. Sedation has already been reduced quite significantly.

While we have all been in waiting, now is even a truer waiting time. We wait patiently on the Lord, and as we wait, this is a crucial time for prayer. Our prayers are for peace as we wait, and for Todd to have a full neurological recovery, and that his mind and body will function on his own. We need and appreciate your prayers more than we can express.

The book *Jesus Calling* instructs us to relax in his healing, holy Presence. We are to be still while allowing Him to transform our hearts and minds. When we let go of cares and worries, then we can receive His peace. We can cease striving and know that He is God. Through knowing Him intimately we can become like him. This requires spending time alone with Him, letting go, relaxing, being still, and knowing that He is God.

Psalm 46:10: *Cease striving and know that I am God; I will be exalted among the nations, I will be exalted in the earth.*

—Day 3, Update 2 - June 2, 3:56 p.m.

Toddy has been working pretty hard this

afternoon. Wow! He has been opening his eyes and stirring around. As far as his labs and progress go, he is moving forward.

Our God has been working hard, too, and we know you all have been praying. All this hard work is paying off. Todd's sedation

21

drip has been completely stopped, and now we are waiting for the medication to completely leave his system.

While he has been moving his head, brows, mouth, arms, legs, shoulders, and opening his eyes, we still have an important prayer: that Todd will show us "meaningful" or "purposeful" movement. He still has to show us that he can hear us, understand us, and then physically follow a direction, such as, "Open your eyes, close your eyes" or "Show me your thumbs." Please pray that Todd will gain purposeful movement.

Psalm 67:1-2: *May God be gracious to us and bless us and make his face shine on us—so that your ways may be known on earth, your salvation among all nations.*

Let us have faith in God, in His great power, and in His grand plans.

Chapter 3
My Active Lifestyle

All my life I have liked to be out doing stuff around the farm and lumber yard, so it should come as no surprise that I was pretty much jogging in bed as Meg describes below.

CaringBridge Update—Day 4, June 3, 1:19 p.m.

We only have a quick report this afternoon. Todd has still been moving around quite a bit, even more than yesterday. He moves his legs, toes, arms, head, eyes, and hips a bit. However, we are still looking for purposeful movement and response. He has yet to squeeze anyone's hands when requested to do so.

At this point, the sedation is probably completely flushed from his system. He has been active a lot of the time, and we don't know how much rest he is getting. His recent labs and chest x-ray came back good, and he was taken off of his blood pressure medication and is doing well without it.

Our current concerns and prayer requests are that Toddy will gain great strength and power to his body and brain from our Almighty God so he can show the doctors purposeful response.

Pray also that Todd will be able to digest the nutrients from his feeding tube as he was not able to absorb the amount his nurse was hoping for.

Pray that when the time comes, the neurological assessments and EEGs will go smoothly, measure accurately, and ultimately prove the miracles from the hand of God.

Pray that we, family and friends, will be washed over with a new, overwhelming hope and faith in the goodness and power of the Lord.

Lastly, pray that the medical team will be guided by God's hand.

We are overwhelmed with thanks that God has already given Todd such strength. He has continued to lead Todd forward throughout this entire situation. Again, the family has appreciated the outpouring of encouragement, support, and care this week.

We also have to say that each step through this has presented a more critical time for prayer, and this new stage of Todd's recovery is no different. Now is the time we pray more fervently than ever. Now is the time to petition and intercede for our lovely, wonderful Toddy.

Psalm 66: 1-2, 20: *Shout for joy to God, all the earth!*
Sing the glory of His name; make His praise
glorious.... Praise be to God, who has not rejected
my prayer or withheld His love from me.

—Day 5 - June 4, 2015, 5:00 p.m.

Today we have great news! Thank you, Jesus! After an MRI and EEG, we met with Todd's neurologist. The MRI showed no significant *structural* damage to Todd's brain. Praise the Lord! The MRI showed that the vision area of his brain may have some damage, but this will result in minimal consequence to Todd. Praise the Lord! The EEG showed no seizure activity. Praise the Lord!

The EEG showed slowed brain *activity*, which means there has been some brain injury, but only time will tell the extent of this injury. The EEG also showed heightened responsive brain activity when they shined a light in his eyes and stimulated him. Praise the Lord!

Todd has had more reactive movement in his eyes and more spontaneous activity. Praise the Lord!

However, he has not yet shown purposeful response (the "show me your thumbs" type of activity). This is what we need to see next. This is our prayer and our plea.

While waiting, we pray. Our intercession and petitions are important and matter to God. He cares for us. He cares deeply for Todd. This is the most critical time for prayer. "We covet your prayers," says Faith.

God's loving power and healing touch is what Todd needs in the next 48 hours and beyond. This is our prayer: that God's strength would continue sustaining Todd in miraculous ways, that Todd will have progression every single day, and that he will show the medical team meaningful movement in the next 48 hours.

We will soon post a prayer chain schedule here for family, friends, and strangers to sign up to pray for Todd and these specific requests in half hour increments over the next 48 hours. If you are looking to help the family out, this is our request of you all. Psalm 130: *Out of the depths I cry to you, Lord; Lord,*

> *hear my voice. Let your ears be attentive to my cry for mercy. If you, Lord, kept a record of sins, Lord, who could stand? But with you there is forgiveness, so that we can, with reverence, serve you. I wait for the Lord, my whole being waits, and in his word I put my hope. I wait for the Lord more than watchmen wait for the morning, more than watchmen wait for the morning. Israel, put your hope in the Lord, for with the Lord is unfailing love and with him is full redemption. He himself will redeem Israel from all their sins.*

PRAYER CHAIN SCHEDULE FOR TODD
06/04/15—06/06/15

This is our prayer during these next critical 48 hours: that God's strength will continue sustaining Todd in miraculous ways, that Todd will have progression every single day, and that he will show the medical team meaningful movement on command within the next 48 hours.

Below is the prayer chain schedule for Todd. Please comment below with your name and desired time slot(s). Please and thank you for your prayers. We cannot fully express our gratitude to the Lord for the opportunity to intercede and petition to Him and to you all for your willingness to join us in this prayer movement for Todd.

Philippians 4:4-7: *Rejoice in the Lord always. I will say it again: Rejoice! Let your gentleness be evident to all. The Lord is near. Do not be anxious about anything, but in every situation, by prayer and petition, with thanksgiving, present your requests to God. And the peace of God, which transcends all understanding, will guard your hearts and your minds in Christ Jesus.*

Thursday, 06/04/15

6:30 p.m. - Leisa Meggison, Sue Logeman

7:00 p.m. - Ashley de Lima, Christin Jalali

7:30 p.m. - Troy and Angela Peterson, Anne Brigham

8:00 p.m. - Sharon Bortz

8:30 p.m. - Sharon Bortz

9:00 p.m. - Sid and Patricia Short, Aaron Baker family, Cheryl Thorrez, Dick and Ann Hensel, Ray Curtis Family, F and H Grogg, Lana Collver, Dwight and Karen Kingsbury, Joy Bortz, Cathy DeVisser, Mason family, Jessica Daugherty, Linda VanValin, Clingers, Bill and Shirley Powers

9:30 p.m. - Rebecca Shaw

10:00 p.m. - Josh Bean, Bert Mercer, Jody Reynolds, Kendra St John

10:30 p.m. - Leigh Ganton, Veronica Vandenburgh, Marie Ermold

11:00 p.m. - Charity Forte Bean, Jean O'Brien

11:30 p.m. - Jim Larrison, Tim Bortz

Friday, 06/05/15

12:00 a.m. - Dave Kamke, Tony Amstutz, Tricia Amstutz Murdock, Melody Cotterman

12:30 - James Bean

1:00 a.m. - Rhonda Owens, Greg and Henrietta Gilbertson, Sara Kostyu

1:30 a.m. - Greg and Henrietta Gilbertson

2:00 a.m. - Kathy Colton

2:30 a.m. - Kathy Colton

3:00 a.m. - Kathy Colton

3:30 a.m. - Kathy Colton

4:00 a.m. - Judy Lyon, Tom Reynolds, Marie Ermold

4:30 a.m. - Cheryl Thorrez, William Kingsbury, Carol Seldon, Tim Comden, Rita Dawson, Chester Chan

5:00 a.m. - Kathy Riggleman, Gwen Hersha, Don Roush, Bob Kintigh

5:30 a.m. - Debra Holton, Anna Hicks

6:00 a.m. - Margie Upton, Troy Peterson, Lynda Riske Wooden, April Barrett, Jayne Asbury

6:30 a.m. - Robin Bortz, Mary Campbell, Don Mercer,

7:00 a.m. - Sharon Bortz, Connie Fenton, Pat Burbridge, Aaron Baker family, Joyce Amstutz, Courtney Ganton

7:30 a.m. - Anita Whitney, Wendy Grant, Marie Ermold, Mary Ann Ayling

8:00 a.m. - Muriel Bortz, Jerry Muterspaugh,

8:30 a.m. - Troy and Angela Peterson, Bill Malenke

9:00 a.m. - Cheryl Thorrez, Stan and Majorie Mitts, William Kingsbury, Amy Shanks, Earl and Elma Habecker, Marie Jalali, Melody Kuntzleman, Clingers, John DeLancey

9:30 a.m. - Monte Shanks, Tammie Kingsley Brown

10:00 a.m. - Tricia Amstutz Murdock, Torrey Amstutz, Pedro de Lima, Linda VanValin, Bob, Mary Ann, Ann, and John Broda, Amy Winget

10:30 a.m. - Shelley Amstutz

11:00 a.m. - Dick and Ann Hensel, Wanda Schulcz

11:30 a.m. - Barbara Miller, Kendra St John

12:00 p.m. - Melody Cotterman, Brian Philson, Shellie
Powers

12:30 p.m. - Teri Lively, Joyce Kingsley Thompson,
Tom Kilgore, Rick Van Wagoner, Deb Roush,
Steve Larson, Christopher Thorrez, Sherrie Clark,
Simon Hodgson, Beverly Nikerle, Robert and
Kimberly Moore-Jumonville

1:00 p.m. - Kaitlyn Granger, Carolyn Moyer

1:30 p.m. - Emily Philson, Samuel and Jerry Moyer,
Mike Neel

2:00 p.m. - Amber Knapp, Gerrilee Lacy, Bethany
Bean, Nikki Ganton, John Manthei, Joy Gebhardt

2:30 p.m. - Alicia Collette

3:00 p.m. - Libby Ellis

3:30 p.m. - Beth Kuntzleman, Adrian Frain, Pam
Gregory

4:00 p.m. - Judy Lyon, Tricia Amstutz Murdock, Angie
Grube

4:30 p.m. - Cheryl Thorrez, Marty Briner

5:00 p.m. - Dave and Cindy Kingsbury

5:30 p.m. - John DeLancey, Donna Bentle

6:00 p.m. - Muriel Bortz

6:30 p.m. - Sue Logeman

7:00 p.m. - Trina Amstutz Sheppard family, Brad and Laurie Buter, Bill and Terri Pardee, Jamie and Stu Malcolm

7:30 p.m. - Trina (Amstutz) Sheppard family

8:00 p.m. - Brian Philson, Bill and Terri Pardee

8:30 p.m. - Cathy Murdock, Nancy Sparks

9:00 p.m. - Dwight and Karen Kingsbury

9:30 p.m. - Linda Whiteley Smith, Chris Ropp

10:00 p.m. - Jody Reynolds, Bert Mercer

10:30 p.m. - Veronica Vandenburgh, Charity Bean, Jayne Asbury, Shellie Powers

11:00 p.m. - Jean O'Brien, Sharon Bortz, Rebecca Shaw, James Bean , Marie Ermold

11:30 p.m. - Jaime Teichmer, Scott Parks, Julie Morse

Saturday, 06/06/15

12:00 a.m. - Dave Kamke

12:30 a.m. - Jaime Teichmer, Sara Kostyu

1:00 a.m. - Jaime Teichmer

1:30 a.m. - Emily Philson, Jerry Moyer

2:00 a.m. - Kathy Colton, Carolyn Moyer

2:30 a.m. - Kathy Colton, Carolyn Moyer

3:00 a.m. - Kathy Colton, Carolyn Moyer

3:30 a.m. - Kathy Colton, Carolyn Moyer

4:00 a.m. - Tom Reynolds, Judy Lyon

4:30 a.m. - Amber Knapp, Megan Stephenson, Marie Ermold

5:00 a.m. - Kathy Riggleman, Tim Zeller

5:30 a.m. - Ginny Hannen, William Hubbard, Trina Amstutz Sheppard family

6:00 a.m. - Lynda Riske Wooden, Bob Kintigh

6:30 a.m. - Mary Campbell, Marie Ermold

7:00 a.m. - Sharon Bortz, Carolyn Moyer, Nicki Quine, Joyce Amstutz

7:30 a.m. - Earl and Elma Habecker, Lynn Briner French, Tricia Amstutz Murdock, Mary Ann Ayling, Mary Wendell Collver,

8:00 a.m. - Amy Winget, Jerry Muterspaugh, Norm Amstutz

8:30 a.m. - Faith McClung Kline O'Brien

9:00 a.m. - Clingers, Sue DeLancey

9:30 a.m. - Rick Van Wagoner, Patricia Smith

10:00 a.m. - Wendy Huff, Monte and Amy Shanks, Panama Ladies Prayer Group (Lisa Amstutz)

10:30 a.m. - Cassidy Losey, Haley Williams

11:00 a.m. - Cassidy Losey, Marie Ermold

11:30 a.m. - Lauren Daigle, Barb Coleman, Gene and Marylou Habecker, Clint Rothell, Vince and Bonita Bridge, Karen Bockwitz, Muriel Bortz,

Miriam Sailers, Jan Yeaman, Susan Tyler, Wendy Warbritton, Laura Hall, Amber McKee, Doyle and Darlene Kingsbury Perry

12:00 p.m. - Rita Dawson, Sue DeLancey, Jeanette Acker, Miriam Sailers, Jan Yeaman

12:30 p.m. - Joyce Kingsley Thompson

1:00 p.m. - Jayne Asbury, Bonnie Bauman, Joy Yambor, Caryn Brandonisio, Ray Curtis family, Lorna Angus

1:30 p.m. - Gary Cayton, Linda and Ron Schaub, Lorna Angus

2:00 p.m. - Joy Gebhardt, Esther Yordy

2:30 p.m. - Lauren Prout, Annalisa Brigham

3:00 p.m. - Morlock family, Denise and Chuck Tomasello

3:30 p.m. - Tricia Amstutz Murdock

4:00 p.m. - Judy Lyon, Josh and Abby Soper

4:30 p.m. - Morlock family, Beverly Clark Winchell

5:00 p.m. - Dave and Cindy Kingsbury

5:30 p.m. - Paige, Kathleen, and Dave Marken

6:00 p.m. - Carolee Hamilton, Cheryl Trepus, Gary and Jann Allan

6:30 p.m. - Connie Fenton, Marie Ermold

We are also profoundly grateful for the unknown number of people who did not sign up for the prayer chain but who were still praying fervently for Todd's healing. After all has been said and done, we are taught by Jesus to pray in private.

Chapter 4

The Power of Prayer

Todd here, speaking some months after the prayer chain was formed. I can't begin to tell you how grateful I am to Linda VanValin for suggesting a prayer chain. Just four weeks earlier our church body prayed for Tim Davidson who had been in a devastating auto accident. His daily updates and prayer chain were posted on *CaringBridge*. So my daughter-in-law Meg organized the same thing for me. I believe in the power of prayer, and I'd like to tell you about an amazing answer to prayer I had previously experienced.

One July in the 1990s before cell phones and GPS and precise weather data, I was driving a combine to harvest wheat in a 20-acre field behind my dad's house that boarders the Kalamazoo River. I had our 1086 International tractor parked at the south end of the field with two gravity-style feed wagons hooked up to it. This was the same field where, years earlier, Grandpa and I flipped the loaded corn wagons. In fact, come to think of it, what I'm about to relate happened at the same spot. I was driving our 6600 John Deere combine, and as I was cutting the wheat headed north, I noticed an ominous wall of black clouds coming out of the west. I knew I was in trouble—it was going to rain! I wanted to finish that round and dump the wheat and get back to the barn before the rain.

The first wagon was full of wheat and I was attempting to fill the second wagon. Soon I saw raindrops on the windshield. I stopped the combine, opened the door, held my hand up, and felt small raindrops falling. I prayed, "Lord, this is your wheat, and I am praying in faith, and in earnest, that you won't let it rain until I finish this round and get the wheat in the barn." I got back in the cab and started to finish that round.

By the time I got to the end of the field and turned around, and started to head south to the tractor and wagons, I could see that the black wall of clouds was almost to the field in the west. As I turned and looked behind me, it was just as black to the east. Then I looked north and saw it was black and raining. And yet, as I looked straight above me, I saw clear blue sky.

I got to the end of the field, dumped the wheat into the second gravity wagon—about 150 bushels—shut the combine off, jumped into the tractor cab, and headed for the barn. The sky to the south was gray, but not raining. The barn door was open and I pulled the tractor and both wagons right straight into the barn. As I shut the tractor off and was closing the barn doors, it began pouring. Instantly I started to cry, thanking God for answered prayer.

Although I was unconscious during the 48-hour prayer vigil, my family and friends know these stories and believe strongly in prayer. It's no surprise to me that many folks firmly believed their prayers on my behalf would be answered when Meg posted on *CaringBridge* that they would hold this 48-hour prayer vigil.

CaringBridge Update—Day 6 – June 5, 3:50 p.m.

Praise God from whom all blessings flow! We have been praying for Todd to show daily progress and daily improvements. Today this is what we have witnessed. When the neurologist visited Todd and lowered his sedative, Todd became more alert, opened and closed his eyes upon command, and smiled real big at his nurse. He also lifted his arm when his nurse asked him to, and he responded to the neurologist's pain stimulus.

After hearing our voices, he turned to each of us and made eye contact with us, then showed us emotion. Our prayers up until this point have moved God's healing hand, and this is just the beginning on the road to complete healing.

While these steps are huge and encouraging, we know that prayer is still the critical key in Todd's complete healing. The family has been overwhelmed at the number of people who filled the prayer chain schedule so quickly. This good, good, news does not change the intense need for prayer.

We are continuing to pray that Todd will show purposeful movement in his extremities, that he will continue daily progress neurologically, and that his body, mind, and spirit will experience the healing hand of God.

The family cannot express the appreciation and deep gratitude to our good, good God and to all of the family, friends, and strangers who have committed to being a part of Todd's road to recovery. Your prayers are of the utmost importance.

Psalm 91: *Whoever dwells in the shelter of the Most High will rest in the shadow of the Almighty. I will*

say of the Lord, "He is my refuge and my fortress,
my God, in whom I trust." Surely he will save you
from the fowler's snare and from the deadly
pestilence. He will cover you with his feathers, and
under his wings you will find refuge; his
faithfulness will be your shield and rampart. You
will not fear the terror of night, nor the arrow
that flies by day, nor the pestilence that stalks in
the darkness, nor the plague that destroys at
midday. A thousand may fall at your side, ten
thousand at your right hand, but it will not come
near you. You will only observe with your eyes and
see the punishment of the wicked. If you say, "The
Lord is my refuge," and you make the Most High
your dwelling, no harm will overtake you, no
disaster will come near your tent. For he will
command his angels concerning you to guard you
in all your ways; they will lift you up in their
hands, so that you will not strike your foot against
a stone. You will tread on the lion and the cobra;
you will trample the great lion and the serpent.
"Because he loves me," says the Lord, "I will rescue
him; I will protect him, for he acknowledges my
name. He will call on me, and I will answer him; I
will be with him in trouble, I will deliver him and

honor him. With long life I will satisfy him and show him my salvation."

Chapter 5
Friends in High Places

My friends in Spring Arbor were not the only people who prayed. I have a lot of friends in Haiti, having made 15 trips to help the church there. Mainly I am involved with building projects at the churches and schools. I also work with the goat project. We ear-tag each of the new goats, write their numbers down, vaccinate them for worms, and trim their hoofs.

This is like a medical clinic for goats, and all the locals bring their animals to the church for treatment. My friend Marv DeVisser heads up this project to help Haitians become a little more self-sufficient by providing milk and meat for their families.

The Park Christian Church was our home base in Haiti. Pastor Devariste Elidor was a driving force in leading that church, and we had become friends.

North American Free Methodist Bishop David Roller grew up in Spring Arbor and I've known him since elementary school. He later married Yvonne Johnston whose mother, Oletha Johnston, led me to

the Lord when I was nine years old during junior
church in the Spring Arbor Free Methodist Old Stone
Church. Another important influence was custodian
Guy Priest used to let a few of us young men ring the
church bell before Sunday service by pulling on the
long rope. [Old Stone Church painting by Paul Wolber]

Bishop David and Pastor Devariste both knew
me well, but neither of them knew that the other
knew me. During my brush with death Bishop Roller
was in Haiti to commission Pastor Devariste as Haiti's
first bishop—for they had just become their own
General Conference.

The commissioning was set to take place on
Friday morning, June 5, at the Park Christian Free
Methodist Church in Port Au Prince. Between 2,000

and 3,000 people had gathered for the ceremony. As Bishop Roller was about to lay hands on Pastor Devariste to commission him, Pastor Devariste said, "Wait! Before this happens, we need to pray for *Mr. Thad.*"

Bishop Roller was perplexed because he has a son named Thaddeus, and he said, "We can pray for my son if you want, but I'm not sure why."

Pastor Devariste said, "No, not your son, but Mr. *Thad.* Mr. *Thad!*"

"Oh!" Bishop David said. "Do you mean "Mr. *Todd* who is in the hospital back in Michigan?"

"Yes! Mr. *Thad!*"

I am very moved when I think that on this great day of commissioning Haiti's first Free Methodist Bishop, Pastor Devariste, being the man of God he is and sensing the importance of the Lord's work, felt it was more urgent to pray for me than for them to pray for him in the commissioning service.

Praying for me was Pastor Devariste' s last pastoral act before being installed as bishop. I will be forever indebted to my thousands of Haitian brothers and sisters in Christ who prayed for me.

It's not often that we see behind the curtain of God's handiwork orchestrating miracles and answers to prayer.

On February 21, 2016, I returned to Haiti and gave a warm thank you and told my story to the Parc Christian Church. You can view my talk on Facebook SAFMC Haiti 2016.

Caring Bridge **Update**

—Day 7 - June 6, 2015, 3:51p.m.

Todd has had an active day! This morning his sedation was lowered significantly so he could be more alert. The medical team emphasized the importance of strictly limiting the number of visitors. He was moved from his hospital bed to a large hospital chair for about an hour so he could have a change of scenery.

Today Todd has continued to show spontaneous movement, recognize voices, and track voices. He seems to want to hold our hands, he shows some emotions, and he took direction from the nurse to stop his restless moving while sitting in the chair. His neurologist is glad to see his progress and is quite optimistic about the next couple of days for Todd.

Still, his ventilator tube bothers him. His critical care intensivist has consulted with a surgeon regarding having a peg tube and tracheotomy put in next week if Todd still needs supplementary nutrition and oxygen.

Our desire is for Todd to consistently breathe on his own without ventilator support so as to avoid tracheotomy surgery. Either way, the medical team believes that when he can get the tube out of his throat, he will be more comfortable and it will help to facilitate recovery. Also, the removal of the tube will help our chatty Todd to catch up on gabbing!

We are grateful for another day marking progress. What a joy!

Continued prayer requests are for Todd to have consistent purposeful movement in his extremities; for him to have sufficient independent breathing; for his discomfort and agitation to be minimal as he is weaned off sedation and becomes more aware of his surroundings; and for God to sustain and strengthen both Todd and us through the next couple of critical days.

A flower bouquet arrived today accompanied by this poem:

You are My beloved child. Out of My own self I have created you. My life is your life; My breath is your breath; My spirit is your spirit. There is nothing to fear, for I am with you, mighty in the midst of you.

I am the life that heals you. I am the love that lifts your heart and set you free. I am the wisdom of your mind. I am the light of your path. I am the peace of your soul.

I am with you, dear child, through every hour of the day and the night, standing with you, upholding you, supporting you, revealing Myself to you and through you.

I am the love that will not let you go. I seek you out when you do not know how to reach Me. I speak in your heart to comfort you. I am the life of your body, and My life is perfect and eternal. Trust Me. I am your health.

I am with you and all the experiences of your life. I am the power in you to understand; I am the power in you to forgive; I am the power in you to become.

Beloved, I am with you. Live in Me. Rejoice in Me. You are My beloved child.

—Day 8 - June 7, 4: 14 p.m.

Early this morning marked a week since Todd came into the hospital. This past week has been the fastest, yet longest week we've ever experienced. As we look back over this past week, and even before, we have seen God's hand over Todd, the family, and the medical team.

Today marks another day of trusting in the Lord and waiting for healing. We have witnessed answered

prayers: progression of Todd's pu[...]
on command of his extremities an[...]
Praise God! Honestly, we know it i[...]
all the prayers that sustain and str[...]
the family.

Our [...]
conti[...]

We have also started to look a[...]
week and what it may have in store for Todd.
Tomorrow the electro-physiologist and the
cardiologist will consult together and give a
recommendation for when Todd should have the
internal cardiac defibrillator (ICD) implanted.

Upon consultation between the intensivist,
cardiologist, neurologist, pulmonologist, thoracic
surgeon, and electro-physiologist, it is anticipated
that on Tuesday, Todd will have his endotracheal
tube (ventilator tube down his throat through his
mouth) replaced with a tracheostomy tube and will
have a PEG tube (feeding tube into stomach) put in.

The medical team is also looking at the end of
this week to transfer Todd from the CCU at
Allegiance, which is an acute care facility, into a sub-
acute rehabilitation facility. His ICD procedure may
precede his transfer or he may return to the hospital
after time spent in rehab to have this done.

...praises for this Sabbath day are that Todd ...nues to have progression in purposeful ...ovement upon command, and that his clinical health remains stable and healthy. Also, we are most grateful for a medical team that has been encouraging, loving, and supportive!

Prayer requests for today are that Todd's steady progression will continue; that the medical team, with the many consultations and decisions this week, will have wisdom and guidance that only come from God; that Todd's children will be refreshed with peace and will be able to focus as they return to their responsibilities and places of employment; and that Faith will be refreshed with the strength of the Lord as she faces many decisions and as she continues to stand at Todd's side.

Psalm 46:1-2, 7, and 10: *God is our refuge and strength, an ever-present help in trouble. Therefore we will not fear, though the earth give way and the mountains fall into the heart of the sea....The Lord Almighty is with us; the God of Jacob is our fortress.... He says, "Be still, and know that I am God; I will be exalted among the nations, I will be exalted in the earth."*

—Day 9, June 8, 2015, 5:57 p.m.

Hope, faith, patience, and peace are characteristics of the Holy Spirit. These are the very things we've longed for in the past week, and the very things that have been renewed in us. The Holy Spirit has been clearly present and we have seen the healing power of God already through Todd's recovery. We have been overwhelmed at God's goodness and grace, Todd's tenacity, and our family and friends' outpouring of love and support.

Yesterday we asked God to powerfully intervene in Todd's body and mind to allow Todd's steady progression to continue exponentially. The Lord answered this prayer very specifically. Yesterday morning and early afternoon Todd's purposeful responses were quite limited. However, by last night and this morning, Todd's progression took a significant turn for the better.

Since last night, Todd has been able to blink his eyes, squeeze and release his hands, wiggle his toes, raise his hands, and show thumbs-up on command. He has also been able to nod and shake his head in response to some questions. Last night this activity was considered purposeful movement, but today it is considered *consistent* purposeful movement. He is a fighter and God is a fighter. As we told him this morning, "You and Jesus are blowing everyone out of the water!"

As for the rest of Todd's recovery, his cardiologist informed us that he will be doing an echocardiogram (ultrasound of the heart) either today or tomorrow to measure the function of Todd's heart. The results of this echocardiogram will affect the decision about implanting the ICD, internal cardiac defibrillator.

The electro-physiologist (cardiologist specializing in heart rhythm disorders) also stopped by this afternoon. He has made the recommendation that if Todd is to have the ICD implanted, that he have the procedure after the tracheotomy and PEG tube procedures tomorrow, but before he is transferred to a sub-acute rehabilitation facility.

Todd is scheduled to have a tracheostomy tube and PEG tube procedure on Tuesday at 4:00 p.m. Earlier today, after seeing Todd's alertness and his ability to make purposeful movements on command, Todd's pulmonologist (physician specialized in lung conditions) considered extubating (removing his endotracheal ventilator tube from his throat) him today.

However, because he has bilateral pneumonia (in both lobes), the medical team decided that it was in Todd's best interest for them to look at the possibility of extubation tomorrow morning instead. So, they will take a look tomorrow to see if he is in a well enough state for extubation. If not, he will go ahead with his scheduled tracheotomy surgery tomorrow afternoon.

This Monday afternoon has presented quite a few prayer requests. We know that God answers prayer, not only because we've read and heard of his mercies, but because we have witnessed and seen his mercies firsthand.

We pray that God will continue to move Todd toward full recovery with steady progression improving exponentially each day; in his lungs, heart, brain, and body.

We pray that Todd's pneumonia will continue to clear at a steady and speedy rate.

We pray that the echocardiogram performed later today or tomorrow will measure accurately and show God's healing in Todd's heart function.

We pray that if Todd must have any procedures this week, that God's hand will be the guide through each procedure.

We also pray, as Todd continues to have increased alertness and awareness of his current state and surroundings, that he will be washed over with the peace, confidence, and strength which only comes from the Lord God.

Romans 8:31-39: *What, then, shall we say in response to these things? If God is for us, who can be against us? He who did not spare his own Son, but gave him up for us all—how will he not also, along with him, graciously give us all things? Who will bring any charge against those whom God has chosen? It is God who justifies. Who then is the one who condemns? No one. Christ Jesus who died—more than that, who was raised to life—is at the right hand of God and is also interceding for us. Who shall separate us from the love of Christ? Shall trouble or hardship or persecution or famine or nakedness or danger or sword?*

As it is written: "For your sake we face death all day long; we are considered as sheep to be slaughtered."

No, in all these things we are more than conquerors through him who loved us. For I am convinced that neither death nor life, neither angels nor demons, neither the present nor the future, nor any powers, neither height nor depth, nor anything else in all creation, will be able to separate us from the love of God that is in Christ Jesus our Lord.

Chapter 6
Meanwhile In My Brain

The prayers for my increasing alertness were certainly answered. I came in and out of consciousness quite a bit, and it was about this time that the following took place—whether in the body or out of the body I can't say.

In that comatose state I remember sitting on a piano bench next to our former music minister David Rupert. He looked really, really good—young, vibrant—with no wrinkles and no glasses. I didn't know him at that age, but he was a younger man.

Around David I could see the keyboard but no piano was visible because of a brilliant white light that surrounded him and where the piano would be—it was all around us. This reminded me of

the same brilliant white that I had experienced before. It was May in the mid-1980s and I was planting corn in fields east of my dad's house. The field ran north and south, and I was turned around, heading back south toward Sears Road. I was somewhat daydreaming about what it must be like to be in heaven, and all at once I happened to look up.

When you're planting corn you have to pay attention—you have to look right down the center of your radiator cap that lines up with the marker in the dirt that the marker arm makes every time you pass for the next round of corn.

My grandfather always said, "Keep the row straight." But in spite of all my careful attention, at some point I happened to look up and saw two huge clouds moving from the southwest to the northeast. It was like they were chasing each other, and just touching and bumping each other. The leading cloud stopped and the cloud that was chasing it stopped and backed up, and what I saw was two walls that came to a 90 degree corner facing me. As the clouds separated, the two walls went in either direction, one to the south and one to the east, and they disappeared into the two clouds.

The wall had twelve huge rows of blocks, one on top of the other, and the corner where it came together—instead of being right straight up square—protruded forward at the bottom like the reverse bow of a ship. The base of the wall was closest to me and succeeding rows were stepped back all the way to the top.

On top of this wall a huge dome sat that was whiter than the white clouds. This whole structure was incredibly white and bright, and yet I could look at it.

In amazement, I stopped the tractor, put it in neutral, and raised my hands toward the sky. Tears poured down my face as I thanked God for what I believe was a vision of heaven. Time stood still. I don't have any idea how long I was stopped—whether a few seconds or minutes—but pretty soon the two clouds moved back together and the vision of heaven was gone.

More than 20 years later I asked Bethany Posa, an art graduate of Spring Arbor University, to help me recreate that scene. Her painting is on the front cover of this book. It's very difficult to paint white on white on white, so Bethany chose to use some yellow hues to give it the feeling of the sun. The painting can't be accurate because the intensity of this bright white on white on white transcends the color spectrum.

All that to say, I understood the white, bright light surrounding David Rupert at the heavenly piano because I had seen it before.

David was playing a fast tune and smiling—a tune I knew from my childhood, but I can't put a name to it. He was a classical music kind of guy. He reveled more in the hymns and didn't have a lot of super-fast stuff, but this one was fast. I just remember feeling really, really good. I was in a good place. David's skin was his normal color, and his hair was dark. He wasn't wearing wings or a white robe, he was just looking right at me while he was playing. I just remember thinking, "this is so cool!"

When I talked with his widow, Ruth, several days after I was home, I told her I had seen David. Her first question to me was, "How did he look?"

I said to Ruth, "He looked great!" She had a picture of him in a military uniform on the bookshelf when he would have been much younger, and the look on his face was similar to what I remember from my visitation with him.

I told her about that fast song he was playing. She said, "Just a minute" and went off to find the *Rupert Family Favorites CD*. She gave it to me and said, "Listen to number 11." As soon as I got home, I put it in my player, and that was the song he was playing: "Onward Christian Soldiers, marching On to War." This was a grand, alive, upbeat version of the song—he was up and down that keyboard!

I've just now started reading *90 Minutes in Heaven* and have found similarities to what that author describes. I can't say for certain that I was actually in heaven, but things like the music, the peace, and the bright white light are what I experienced while I was unconscious. It was a very peaceful place.

CaringBridge Update
—Day 10 - June 9, 2015 , 9:26 a.m.

Todd's typical morning starts out with a bite of breakfast and devotional time—often a reading from *Our Daily Bread*. Throughout the past ten days, Todd has been able to get a little of this devotional time when we read to him. This morning the reading referenced Deuteronomy 8 11-18:

*Be careful that you do not forget the Lord
your God, failing to observe his commands, his
laws and his decrees that I am giving you this day.
Otherwise, when you eat and are satisfied, when
you build fine houses and settle down, and when
your herds and flocks grow large and your silver
and gold increase and all you have is multiplied,
then your heart will become proud and you will
forget the Lord your God, who brought you out of
Egypt, out of the land of slavery. He led you
through the vast and dreadful wilderness, that
thirsty and waterless land, with its venomous
snakes and scorpions. He brought you water out of
hard rock. He gave you manna to eat in the
wilderness, something your ancestors had never
known, to humble and test you so that in the end it
might go well with you. You may say to yourself,
"My power and the strength of my hands have
produced this wealth for me." But remember the
Lord your God, for it is he who gives you the ability
to produce wealth, and so confirms his covenant,
which he swore to your ancestors, as it is today.*

The author of today's reading also referenced a story
of a swimmer who took a dip in a bay. He was
impressed with himself because he was able to

navigate well through the water and decided to go out into the open bay. When he tried to return, he was stunned to realize that on his way out into the open water, it was not by his own strength he navigated but because of the currents.

We are humbled at this reminder. God has brought Todd, and us, partway through the valley. It is by the tide of His power, strength, and grace that Todd has had a steady recovery.

Today was a big day for Todd—his tracheotomy and PEG tube surgeries went well without complications. This afternoon, Todd also had an echocardiogram, and we are waiting to hear the report tomorrow. We praise God for caring about Todd so intimately and deeply that he intentionally intervenes every single day.

Our prayer requests now are that Todd's bilateral pneumonia will heal at a steady, speedy rate as this morning's chest x-ray showed his pneumonia has advanced.

Pray that Todd's tracheostomy tube incision will heal well and have no complications.

Pray that the echocardiogram will show the healing power of God and that God's wisdom will guide the decisions regarding the possibility of an ICD implantation.

Pray that the process of weaning away the sedation will be a smooth transition for Todd's mind and body.

We also pray that as Todd continues to have increased alertness and awareness of his current state and surroundings, that he will be washed over with the peace, confidence, and strength which only comes from the Lord God.

I, Meg, want to say thank you to all who scour the site for Todd's updates. While this one comes to you late, we still want to let you all know that we appreciate your prayers and support. We know, truly, how difficult it is to wait for an update. So, thank you for your diligence and for your consistent love.

Chapter 7

"Joya Joya Joya!"

Because of the drugs I was on, the days of the first week run together in my memory. I remember opening my eyes, looking around, and knowing people and my surroundings. I don't think I was aware of being in the hospital, but I was aware of lying in bed and that there were people I knew around me: I remember my wife, my mother, and my sister JoLynne.

The other lady there—who spoke the first words I remember—was my neighbor Marie Sanford. Both of her folks were born in Italy, so she is 100% Italian. I remember her grabbing my face with both of her hands and exclaiming "Joya Joya Joya!"

Then it was a constant barrage of people coming in and out. Pastor Darold Hill and Marge were there almost every day. My brother Kyle and my sons Nathan, Philip, and Thomas were all there.

My wife told me later that Philip had a really hard time at the hospital because he felt he was responsible for keeping me alive, and he was afraid he might not have done everything right. He was not fully sure that I was going to make it and said to my wife, "Why is everybody so optimistic when we don't know if Dad will survive?"

I recently asked my mother, "What was the hardest thing of this whole event for you?"

She said, "As a mother, knowing there was nothing I could do to ease your suffering when you were turning blue in that ice bath."

They slowly took my body temperature down to 91.6—the reverse of a frog in hot water—and I was covered with a light blanket on my chest to keep me from shivering. For Mom to see me in that condition and know she was helpless to do anything but pray was very difficult for her.

CaringBridge Update
—Day 11 - June 10, 10:52 a.m.

Psalm 66:1-6: *Shout for joy to God, all the earth! Sing the glory of his name; make his praise glorious. Say to God, 'How awesome are your deeds! So great is your power that your enemies cringe before you. All the earth bows down to you; they sing praise to you, they sing the praises of your name.' Come and see what God has done, his awesome deeds for mankind! He turned the sea into dry land, they passed through the waters on foot— come, let us rejoice in him.*

Listen, we are indeed shouting for joy and singing the glory of His name this morning! The medical team told us that the tracheostomy tube would make a big difference for Todd and facilitate recovery. This morning, Todd is back in his medical chair and his nurse has shut off his sedation. We were a little apprehensive because it was difficult for him the last time he was completely taken off of sedation.

However, this morning is polar opposite. Todd is smiling, smooching, nodding, and shaking his head. He is very alert and aware. His body is not struggling like it was the other day; it is calm and he has decent muscle control. He recognizes people and waves and smiles at them. His personality is shining through in ways it hasn't in the past eleven days. Praise God!

Todd's recovery up to this point is a testament to the love, grace, and strength poured out on us by God and his many praying people. It is like Todd has finally showed up to say "hi" to us today. He is still unable to talk because of the tracheostomy tube, but he is trying to get words out.

Also, Todd is scheduled to have the ICD (pacemaker) implantation this afternoon at 3:30p.m. We are praising God and rejoicing in a much deeper way this morning. Rejoice with us!

Our prayers are the same as yesterday, plus his scheduled ICD implantation this afternoon.

Grandpa Linford Kingsbury and me on the Gemini roller coaster at Cedar Point.

Chapter 8

A Visit with Grandpa

During this crisis, after all the visitors left and I had a little down time, I had an overwhelming sense that I wanted to call my grandfather. He and I were really good buddies. I think I was about as close to my grandfather as anybody. He was born with a cleft palate that we called a "hare lip," and I was born with a similar anomaly to my upper lip, so we called each other "two hare lips." Besides that, Bill Gilbertson's dog bit me when I was about five, leaving a scar on my upper lip.

My mother's father, Linford Kingsbury, grew up on a farm in Deerfield, Michigan, but he later sought work in Toledo at the Willy's Jeep factory where he was a tool and die welder. He could fix anything. When he retired in 1975, he and my grandma June moved to Concord just over a mile from us. For 20 years, from the time I was age 14 until he died in 1995, we were very close. Family meant a lot to us, and I had lots of grandparents around. But I especially liked Grandpa Linford's stories.

Grandpa told me that when he was a kid they had rescued an orphaned woodchuck, brought it into the house, bottle fed it, and named it Chucky. It became a pet. Several months later they let Chucky outside. It came to the back step every day and Great Grandma Ida fed him. Well, one day, the woodchuck left. They just assumed he ran away or was killed. Several days later, Grandma stepped out on the back porch and thought she saw something moving. Sure enough, it was Chucky. She scolded him like you would a dog or child. She pointed her finger and said, "Chucky, where have you been?!" Chucky crouched down in shame and crept up to the back steps knowing he had stayed away too long.

By the time I got out of high school I was responsible for most of the farm which was a couple hundred acres. Grandpa helped me with the farm. I remember the first time Grandpa pulled up with his car to watch me plant corn. As I was coming up the field, he looked right at me and put his hand straight up, lined up in front of his nose, to signal me to keep the row straight. He helped me a lot around the farm, fixing old machinery. When I went off to Hesston College in Kansas to study production agriculture for a couple years, Grandpa and Dad actually put the crops in and did most of the harvesting.

One day before college, we were picking corn on a fairly hilly field back by the Kalamazoo River. We were cob-picking to put it in the crib and were pulling two gravity wagons of corn with a little International 140—way too small for pulling those wagons when loaded. I was driving and Grandpa was riding on the drawbar behind me, holding onto my seat when we started down a steep hill.

The heavy wagons were pushing us down the hill, and at the bottom I had to choose between going into the fence row or follow the lane where it makes a sharp turn to the right. I made the turn, but the first wagon didn't. As the wagon flipped over, Grandpa jumped off and the spilling corn chased him to the point that he literally jumped the snow fence to escape being buried by the corn. The force bent the tongue, but the wagon remained connected to the tractor.

We looked at each other in amazement and started to laugh. Grandpa said, "Whew! What a ride!" He would have been pushing age 70 at the time he vaulted that fence.

Scripture says that old men will see visions and young men will dream dreams (Joel 2:28 and Acts 2:17). Whether it was a vision or a dream, my experience while I was in a coma was real. When I was unconscious—maybe in those first 12 minutes while I was clinically dead—I saw myself walking up to our farm shop where Grandpa and I had worked endless hours fixing things. I can remember the little wood heater in there so we could work in the winter. His welder is still in the old workshop.

As I walked toward the shop, he came out to meet me—about five feet from the shop. We greeted each other, and I asked, "How ya doing Grandpa?"

He said, "I'm doing fine. How are you?"

I said I was fine, we hugged each other, and I said, "You look good, Grandpa."

We were just there in the moment for a while without having to say anything, and then he asked me about my grandson. He said, "How's Palmer?" (Palmer is a family name after Grandpa's great grandma. We named our second son Philip Palmer Holton.)

I said, "Oh, Grandpa, he's great. You would love him. He's full of energy and 100% boy."

Grandpa had a unique laugh. He would smile, his teeth showing through vividly under his mustache. (We both have always worn a mustache to hide our scarred upper lips.) And he'd kinda throw his head back a little bit as part of his laugh.

So Grandpa smiled and gave his unique laugh. He also always wore a silver watch. After a while he checked his watch and said, "Well, I've gotta get going, but we'll talk again sometime."

"I said, "Ok—I'll see you again." I watched him turn and walk back into the shop. The great big overhead garage door was open (just like in the picture to the right of where he and I are standing on the combine), so I could see right into the shop. He walked back in, and as he walked toward the back of the shop, he just kinda faded away and disappeared.

I turned and walked away. I wasn't sad or anything, it was just as if we had never left each other. That was my vision. When I woke up— whether a day or a week later—I had the sense that I wanted to call him on a phone. But as the afternoon wore on into evening and the drugs began wearing off, I realized I couldn't call him because he's not here. Come to think of it, he's been dead for 20 years. That made me a little sad that I can't call Grandpa.

Then it hit me—what if he'd have asked me to come with him? What if I had taken one step into the shop? What if he had asked me, "Hey, can I show you something?"

I truly believe that if that had happened, he would have ushered me right into heaven. And yet I knew that it wasn't my time. I really think God told him, "Linford, don't ask Todd to come—it's not his time yet."

Grandpa Linford and I had some experience with this question of when our time is coming. You see, after Grandma June died, Grandpa kept on living in the same house by himself. My mother, Aunt Kay, and Uncle Bill came to help him when they could, but most of the daily checking on Grandpa fell on my mom. He wanted to stay in his house as long as he could. It was really wearing on my mom, and I was afraid all this work was going to make her ill.

One day I finally went to Grandpa and said, "I know you want to stay here as long as you can, and I know you've looked at a retirement home, and I really think you should reconsider that. You know that I love you very much, but it's really wearing on Mom. She wants what's best for you and she'll never tell you 'no.'"

When I told him that, he began to cry. Then he said, "I knew this day was coming. I'll call my son Bill tonight and say, "I've changed my mind, and I think it's time for me to move out of the house.'"

We both agreed we didn't want anyone to know we had this conversation. And actually, after he moved into Arbor Oaks in Spring Arbor, he really enjoyed the fellowship of the people there. He appreciated the close proximity to the church, and he told me later, "I should have done this weeks or months earlier."

***CaringBridge* Update**

—Day 11 – Wednesday, June 10, 7:24 p.m.

Lamentations 3:22-26: *Because of the Lord's great love we are not consumed, for his compassions never fail. They are new every morning; great is your faithfulness. I say to myself, "The Lord is my portion; therefore I will wait for him." The Lord is good to those whose hope is in him, to the one who seeks him; it is good to wait quietly for the salvation of the Lord.*

The ICD implantation this afternoon went very well! Thanks to God for intervening and to you all for interceding. God has been answering our prayers so specifically. We are in awe. Todd has also been taken off of sedation and the ventilator completely, though either may be started again if necessary.

Toddy is back, more and more. He is mouthing a lot of words as he cannot yet speak. He is animated and lively. He is trying to communicate a lot—of course! He also recognizes people, knows names, makes jokes, makes his typical facial expressions and gestures, asks persistently for a fan, and is coming around in such a miraculous way.

Now he has completed all of his scheduled procedures. Ahead is the transfer to a sub-acute medical care facility at the end of this week.

Our prayer requests now are for the bilateral pneumonia to continue clearing, for the upcoming swallow test to go well, for the transition from the CCU to the sub-acute medical care facility to go smoothly, and, again, for Todd to continue having a positive attitude, peace, strength, and hope as he recovers and realizes more.

We are overwhelmed today with the turn Todd took, overnight, for the better! He has already had us all smiling and laughing. How good it is to see him! Please continue to pray with us as Todd's road to recovery is just beginning and as he, and we, begin to realize the lifelong adjustments that may need to be made.

Praise God from whom all blessings flow.

—Day 12 - June 11, 9:42 p.m.

We are astounded at the infinite mercies of God. Today has indeed been another day of amazing progress. A few days ago, our request was that God would continue to heal Todd exponentially each day and He has been answering that very prayer. While

Todd cannot yet vocalize his words, he has been mouthing words nonstop, as you all can imagine! He even mouthed *buon natale, gioia, gioia, gioia!*—an Italian expression a dear friend often says. It took us several minutes to figure that one out!

The big news today is that Todd moved from the critical care unit up to the progressive care unit at Allegiance. He is no longer considered in "critical condition." He has continued to be off of sedation and the ventilator. He was very enthusiastic, animated, and positive today and was determined to get out of bed. He was able to sit up at the edge of the bed for a while and then stand up and sit in a regular chair today with minimal assistance from the Occupational Therapist.

While his pneumonia has not gotten better, it has not gotten any worse as of this morning. He has to cough often which is good for him, but requires a lot of energy as well.

We were also updated by one of the nurses that Todd's echocardiogram showed significant improvement of ejection fraction (heart function). When the cardiologist, Dr. Baghal, did the angiogram for Todd at the beginning of last week to discover what may have caused cardiac arrest, it showed his ejection fraction to be 20-25% (the average person's is 50-65%). The echocardiogram a couple of days ago showed that Todd's ejection fraction is now 47%! Praise God, oh my soul!

The Lord's care is so very intimate. We had no idea a week ago, or even the day before yesterday, what today would have done to our souls. Todd's smiles, hugs, jokes, chuckles, humor, tenderness, and strength all washed over us in such an overwhelming way.

Today was another gift from God; Todd Douglas is back—and while he may have missed 11 days, he did not miss a beat! We are truly taken aback at how the God of the universe answers *our* prayers, and at how His body comes together for the sake of one, and therefore many.

The praises to our Father today are *many*. Wow! Honestly, we are speechless (I say "speechless" after I wrote a lengthy update—ha!). Truly, we are astonished.

Prayer requests include that the bilateral pneumonia would not only be held at bay, but would improve.

Pray also that the occupational therapy, physical therapy, and speech therapy (swallow test) assessments will go smoothly and that all involved, including Todd and us, will have a great amount of patience.

Pray that the upcoming decision regarding Todd's next care facility will be drenched in God's wisdom and guidance, as Todd's medical team is now reevaluating his needs (since he is improving so well, so quickly).

Again, pray that Todd will continue to have a positive attitude, peace, strength, and hope as he continues to recover.

Lastly, pray that the family will continue to be sustained by God, to be supported by each other, and to keep leaning on the everlasting arms.

I Chronicles 29:10-13: *David praised the Lord in the presence of the whole assembly, saying, "Praise be to you, Lord, the God of our father Israel, from everlasting to everlasting. Yours, Lord, is the greatness and the power and the glory and the majesty and the splendor, for everything in heaven and earth is yours. Yours, Lord, is the kingdom; you are exalted as head over all. Wealth and honor come from you; you are the ruler of all things. In your hands are strength and power to exalt and give strength to all. Now, our God, we give you thanks, and praise your glorious name."*

Chapter 9

He Walks!

CaringBridge Update
—Day 13 - June 12, 9:15 p.m.

He walks! A physical therapist came to work with Todd today for about 30 minutes. Before we knew it, he was making rounds on his wing of the hospital with a walker.

One of Todd's visitors told him there was a lady down the hall who he knows—Betty Bonney. Naturally, first thing this morning, it was Todd's goal to reach out to Betty. He was bound and determined. He mouthed with tears in his eyes, "Thousands of people have been helping me; I just want to help one—just one!"

And guess what? He did. He took a little walk over to her room, with the help of two medical staff and the walker, and delivered his CD player to his neighbor so she could enjoy some upbeat tunes.

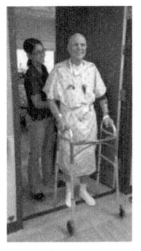 Another one of Todd's great accomplishments today was getting out of bed and into the bathroom, with the assistance of one CNA. He was glad, needless to say. He kept telling people about it all day.

Todd has started to realize more and more what the last 13 days have been like and the amount of support he has received from so many people across the planet. At one point, tears came to his eyes, and he said he was overwhelmed at the many amazing people who have been praying for him. Todd continues to be in good spirits and wore a smile all day. Even at the beginning of visiting hours Todd had his radio blasting with some gospel piano music, dancing around in his bed. While communicating can be at times frustrating since he is still unable to vocalize, he doesn't let that stop him from carrying on conversations with every person who walks in the room.

Word has spread through the hospital about Todd's miraculous recovery. A night nurse from the CCU and the third floor waiting room attendant both came up to visit Todd this evening. The CCU nurse was thrilled at how he has progressed.

We praise the Lord for the way He so uniquely made Todd and the way He so intricately formed this family surrounding him—friends, family, and even strangers.

We are also thankful for Todd's willingness to drop his nets, follow Jesus, and become a fisher of men. He just oozes love and joy and kindness. We are all grateful for the many people who have played a vital part in Todd's recovery thus far—prayer warriors, family, and friends, the wonderful cooks and bakers, the medical team and all of the hospital staff, and ultimately Jesus Christ who is mighty to save in so many different ways.

Things to cover in prayer

The swallow test is still upcoming. It was ordered for today, but did not yet happen. So we pray that this assessment will be finished soon and that it will go well.

The bilateral pneumonia is still the same. We pray that this will start clearing up again.

The next step is still being discussed. We pray that the Lord would continue guiding the conversation and that He will prepare the way, in every aspect, for Todd to be transferred.

The feedings via PEG tube have continued with his transfer to the progressive care unit. We pray that Todd will be able to handle this nutrition without getting sick.

We want to repeat the need for Todd to continue having such a positive attitude, peace, strength, and hope as he recovers and realizes more of what he has experienced.

And again, pray that the family will continue to be sustained by God, to be supported by each other, and to keep leaning on the everlasting arms.

Tonight's scripture passage includes Todd's great grandmother's favorite Bible verse. Today he was quoting it in Swedish, her native language: Isaiah 40:28-31: *Do you not know? Have you not*

> *heard? The Lord is the everlasting God, the Creator of the ends of the earth. He will not grow tired or weary, and His understanding no one can fathom. He gives strength to the weary and increases the power of the weak. Even youths grow tired and weary, and young men stumble and fall; but those who hope in the Lord will renew their strength. They will soar on wings like*

eagles; they will run and not grow weary, they will walk and not be faint.

In Swedish this reads, *Menda sombada dahempta new my croft*—"They that wait upon the Lord shall fetch new power."

—Day 14 – Saturday, June 13, 9:38 p.m.

Today was much like yesterday. It included a walk down his hall, smiles, jokes, tears, laughter, upbeat tunes, many visitors, reminiscing, and long naps. Thank God for another day with several steps in the right direction.

Our prayer requests for tonight are the same as last night as we are still waiting for each of these (especially since it is the weekend).

We pray that the swallow assessment will be finished soon and that it will go well.

We pray that the bilateral pneumonia will start clearing up again.

We pray that the Lord will continue guiding the conversation regarding the next step after Allegiance and that He will prepare the way, in every aspect, for Todd to be transferred.

We pray that Todd will be able to continue handling nutrition without getting sick.

We want to repeat the need for Todd to continue having such a positive attitude, peace, strength, and hope as he recovers and realizes more.

And again, pray that the family will be sustained by God, supported by each other, and to keep leaning on the everlasting arms.

Psalm 18:1-2: *I love you, Lord, my strength. The Lord is my rock, my fortress and my deliverer; my God is my rock, in whom I take refuge, my shield and the horn of my salvation, my stronghold.*

Chapter 10

Awakening Moments

One afternoon I woke up from a dream having to do with Lily Missionary Baptist Church. The odd thing is that from my sixth floor hospital window at Allegiance Hospital in Jackson, I could look out and see south down Page Avenue and look right at the Lily Missionary Baptist Church building.

Seeing that church reminded me of a time when Spring Arbor College called and asked me to build a stage set and some platforms. They were for a homecoming performance by the Dove Award musician and Spring Arbor College graduate, Babbie Mason, who had grown up in that church. Her father, George Wade, pastored that church for many years.

If you want to hear an odd thing about how God

works, think about this: When Babbie was a Spring Arbor student she worked with elementary and middle school students at Concord Public Schools. The room she taught in was next to the middle school gym where Scott Stoner and I taught high school drama.

Each year we directed a school musical, so I visited with Babbie several times. Obviously, I was pleased to be asked to build this set for her. The college called me because for years I had built sets for Esther Maddox and other drama teachers who followed her.

At the Lily Missionary Baptist Church, Babbie wanted a set that would hide the baptismal fount behind the choir loft—she would have a large choir in front of the set. I also built platforms for the video equipment cameras. After several weeks of construction and phone consultations with Babbie, she came to town.

Just a few days before the performance, she was informed by her film producer that the lighting and visuals of this setting were all wrong for creating a high quality production. Babbie felt badly that I had done all this work that would not be used. However, after a few phone calls, the decision was made to move the venue to the Second Baptist Church. I tore down the whole set with the help of some volunteers and we moved the entire set to the new location.

Babbie invited us to the performance, so my wife and I, along with Bob and Barb Delamarter, attended this concert in an all-African American Church. Our four white faces stood out starkly. During this concert, Babbie's mother joined her in singing "God's gonna open up the windows of heaven and pour you out a blessing—and you will not have the room to receive it."

Back in the hospital room, as I lay looking at the Lily Missionary Baptist Church and remembering the dream I just had, that song came to my mind. In an instant I was transported in my dream out of the hospital, hovering above the hospital where I could see the air conditioners and heating units and catwalks, and I could also see outside of the hospital where my sixth floor window was.

I saw a large hand come out of the clouds, reach right over the Lily Missionary Baptist Church, come right through my window, and massage my heart.

I believe this was the hand of God that reached in to massage my heart to keep it going and to help heal it. At the same time, from inside my body, I felt warmth in my heart and healing from God.

CaringBridge Update
—Day 15 - June 14, 8:53 p.m.

A couple of days ago the update said, "He walks!" Today? He talks! Today was the first day in two weeks Todd was able to talk. We are able to hear his familiar voice by using a special speaking valve to cover the outside of his trache so his voice can come out his mouth.

This is a big deal! Todd talks by covering the small hole with his finger so the vocal sounds come out of his mouth and sound normal. But doing that with several visitors makes for an exhausting day. Still, we are stunned and overjoyed with the exponential progress Todd has made. God has been so good to each of us. "It's His breath in our lungs, so we pour praise to Him only."

Tomorrow will be a big day with the continued discussion regarding the next facility for Todd and with the speech therapy assessment which will include the swallow test.

Prayers for tonight are for the elimination of Todd's bilateral pneumonia, the ability for him to handle tube feedings without complication, the upcoming swallow test, Todd's potential transfer to a rehabilitation facility, and strength, patience, and peace for all of us, and especially for Toddy!

Also, know that Todd has been overwhelmed and humbled by the love, support, and prayers you all have poured out in the last two weeks. There is about a 12 day window he does not remember, but he is awe struck to hear of all of the ways people have come alongside all of us and the way God has so intimately been part of each step of every day.

Psalm 100:1-5: *Shout for joy to the Lord, all the earth.*

Worship the Lord with gladness; come before Him with joyful songs. Know that the Lord is God. It is He who made us, and we are His; we are His people, the sheep of His pasture. Enter His gates with thanksgiving and His courts with praise; give thanks to Him and praise His name. For the Lord is good and His love endures forever; His faithfulness continues through all generations.

Chapter 11
Goodbye World, Goodbye!

My wife told me that every day she, my mother, my sister, or others sang to me. They did this in the belief that a person in a coma can hear even if he can't respond. So I believe music played a big role in my recovery. Faith had brought in a portable CD player and they had several different genres of music. The one I enjoyed most was a CD by the late Anthony Berger, a renowned piano player who played with the Gaithers and several quartets through the years. The first number on that CD is a very fast and upbeat song called "Goodbye World, Goodbye."

I listened to that song dozens of times during my stay at the hospital. My wife and friends and hospital staff were probably really tired of it, but while listening to that song, I felt so alive! I could literally feel my blood flowing through my arteries and veins, my oxygen inhaling and exhaling through my lungs—I just tingled with new life. I contribute part of my healing to music therapy.

Now, you should know this: I had made a verbal agreement with the Lord when I left the hospital that if anyone ever asked me to tell my story, that I would be glad to do so. Within a couple days, Dean Boss, who is in charge of scheduling gospel concerts at my church, asked me to give my testimony before a Jim Brady Trio concert.

I spoke before the concert to a crowd of about 400 people. Although the Jim Brady Trio was there, they were in the back room and didn't hear me give my testimony. Halfway through the concert they took a break. "Just before the break," Jim Brady said, "my wife and the pianist will do a piano duet."

The song they played was the very fast-paced "Goodbye World, Goodbye." I looked at my wife, and she looked at me in amazement. Tears ran down my face and we both just smiled.

After the concert, Dean Boss invited a few of us to a dinner and I told Jim Brady and his group how much that song meant for my recovery. I asked if they would do me one last favor after dinner and play that song again. What a special memory. This was just another reassurance from God that He was orchestrating my recovery.

CaringBridge **Update**

—Day 16 - June 15, 9:56 p.m.

Today they moved Todd from the progressive to the Mary Free Bed Rehabilitation floor at Sparrow Hospital in Lansing. The transfer this afternoon went very well. Todd asked the ambulance service EMT if she had heard about his rescue and she said, "Yes, I know the two men who made that run. They weren't sure if you would make it."

[**Note:** Todd thanked her, and when he was out of the hospital he went to their office to thank and shake the hands of those who had saved his life.]

This evening we were given a tour of the new unit and Todd settled into his very nice new room. We were warmly welcomed by various staff members and the resident doctor. Since the transfer happened late this afternoon, no assessments or therapy started tonight. Tomorrow he will hit the ground running with a neuropsychological evaluation, physical therapy, and speech therapy. He will also have a chest x-ray in the morning to check on the status of the bilateral pneumonia.

The medical team's initial thoughts from tonight are quite positive. We are thrilled and are very much looking forward to what this week has in store for him. Interestingly, and perhaps divinely coordinated, Todd has a neighbor across the hall, Tim Davidson, a public school teacher, husband, and father who almost died in a car accident on the way home from work and is now in recovery from traumatic closed head injury.

Tell me, what are the chances? Does our God not ever so intimately and creatively weave the paths of our lives? What an awesome encounter tonight.

Tim stopped by Todd's room tonight, a couple of times. We were all grateful for the blessing of seeing and talking with him. The encounter the two of them had tonight was uniquely beautiful and definitely orchestrated by our loving God. It was unlike anything I (Meg) had every witnessed or experienced.

Seeing them sit next to each other and joining together in prayer was more than moving. The way they just knowingly looked at each other was more than most of us can imagine or fathom. After what they both have been through, they have come far with the Lord sustaining them and with family and friends supporting them. What blessings and praises we pour out to the Lord tonight.

Over the next couple of days we will be praying about the assessments and therapy sessions, the elimination of the bilateral pneumonia, and the ability to continue tube feedings without complication.

Pray for Todd to have a God-given strength, endurance, perseverance, determination, and patience while he transitions to a much more intensive rehabilitation process.

Psalm 115:1: *Not to us, Lord, not to us but to your name be the glory, because of your love and faithfulness.*

CaringBridge Update
—Day 17 - June 16, 9:56 p.m.

What a full day—Todd had bedside physical therapy, speech therapy, occupational therapy, and recreational therapy. Whew! He did very well for his first day and the doctors are impressed with him. They think he'll go through rehabilitation pretty quickly.

Tomorrow will include all of the same therapies as well as a swallow evaluation and further assessments toward removing his trache. He started a cap on the trache tonight and must be able to continue with the cap for at least 24 hours. We all look forward to Todd getting the trache out and the swallow evaluation done. These will be huge steps forward for him.

These are very important prayer requests for tonight and tomorrow, as well as for Todd to continue having strength, hope, joy, and peace that only comes from our loving Lord. Rehab may be a testing time as we all realize more and more what the journey ahead may have in store. We are incredibly grateful for a good first day of therapy. Already we can see a difference.

Psalm 105:1-4: *Give praise to the Lord, proclaim His name; make known among the nations what He has done. Sing to Him, sing praise to Him; tell of all His wonderful acts. Glory in His holy name; let the hearts of those who seek the Lord rejoice. Look to the Lord and His strength; seek His face always.*

—Day 18 - June 17, 8:04 p.m.

The words come to mind, "God's been good to me. Oh, God's always been good." We recently heard someone say that the circumstances in life don't change the goodness of God. While His mysteries are beyond our understanding, trusting in His goodness can carry us through valleys and help us to stand again—sometimes literally. And whether things in life are better or worse, God does not waver under our storms. Rather, the storms can be calmed under our God.

Today's therapies went even better than yesterday. In one session, Todd was able to climb some stairs and take a walk outside. He was stretched and challenged even more today than yesterday. And of course, he was up for it.

We had quite an exciting and eventful afternoon today too. Todd's chest x-ray today showed that his pneumonia has cleared. Praise God! Therefore, his PICC line was removed (a tube that goes through a vein into part of the heart to administer fluids, medications, or to measure pressure).

Todd was able to go through the night and day without any issues related to having the cap on his tracheostomy tube. Therefore, the doctors removed his tracheostomy tube. Praise the good Lord! Because of that, the swallow test was postponed. The PEG tube is the last thing Todd has to get rid of.

We are fervently praying that the swallow test tomorrow goes well. We hope he will be able to swallow without having liquids or other foods go to his lungs so he can start on a food diet. As he will tell you, those warm milkshakes he gets through his PEG tube are no good! They have no flavor because they do not pass the taste buds in his mouth. He is excited about the opportunity to eat again—he has lost about 30 pounds. Please pray with us about the swallow test tomorrow.

Tomorrow morning the medical team will have a conference meeting regarding Todd's case. Todd has progressed by leaps and bounds this week, so tonight and tomorrow we are praying about the swallow test, the medical team meeting, and now the process of looking ahead to Todd's transition out of rehab and into the next step.

We give all the thanks and glory to our mighty God for guiding the healing process that has resulted in clearing Todd's bilateral pneumonia, transferring smoothly to Sparrow, and getting the tracheostomy tube and PICC line out.

2 Corinthians 3:17-18: *Now the Lord is the Spirit, and where the Spirit of the Lord is, there is freedom. And we all, who with unveiled faces contemplate the Lord's glory, are being transformed into His image with ever-increasing glory, which comes from the Lord, who is the Spirit.*

2 Corinthians 4: *Therefore, since through God's mercy we have this ministry, we do not lose heart. Rather, we have renounced secret and shameful ways; we do not use deception, nor do we distort the word of God. On the contrary, by setting forth the truth plainly we commend ourselves to everyone's conscience in the sight of God. And even if our gospel is veiled, it is veiled to those who are perishing. The god of this age has blinded the minds of unbelievers, so that they cannot see the light of the gospel that displays the glory of Christ, who is the image of God. For what we preach is not ourselves, but Jesus Christ as Lord, and ourselves as your servants for Jesus' sake. For God, who said, "Let light shine out of darkness," made his light shine in our hearts to give us the light of the knowledge of God's glory displayed in the face of Christ.*

But we have this treasure in jars of clay to show that this all-surpassing power is from God and not from us. We are hard pressed on every side, but not crushed; perplexed, but not in despair; persecuted, but not abandoned; struck down, but not destroyed.

We always carry around in our body the death of Jesus, so that the life of Jesus may also be revealed in our body. For we who are alive are always being given over to death for Jesus' sake, so that his life may also be revealed in our mortal body. So then, death is at work in us, but life is at work in you. It is written: "I believed; therefore I have spoken."

Since we have that same spirit of faith, we also believe and therefore speak, because we know that the one who raised the Lord Jesus from the dead will also raise us with Jesus and present us with you to himself. All this is for your benefit, so that the grace that is reaching more and more people may cause thanksgiving to overflow to the glory of God.

Therefore we do not lose heart. Though outwardly we are wasting away, yet inwardly we are being renewed day by day. For our light and momentary troubles are achieving for us an eternal glory that far outweighs them all. So we fix our eyes not on what is seen, but on what is unseen, since what is seen is temporary, but what is unseen is eternal.

Psalm 25: *In you, Lord my God, I put my trust. I trust in you; do not let me be put to shame, nor let my enemies triumph over me. No one who hopes in you will ever be put to shame, but shame will come on those who are treacherous without cause. Show me your ways, Lord, teach me your paths. Guide me in your truth and teach me, for you are God my Savior, and my hope is in you all day long. Remember, Lord, your great mercy and love, for they are from of old.*

Do not remember the sins of my youth and my rebellious ways; according to your love remember me, for you, Lord, are good. Good and upright is the Lord; therefore he instructs sinners in his ways. He guides the humble in what is right and teaches them his way. All the ways of the Lord are loving and faithful toward those who keep the demands of his covenant. For the sake of your name, Lord, forgive my iniquity, though it is great.

Who, then, are those who fear the Lord? He will instruct them in the ways they should choose. They will spend their days in prosperity, and their descendants will inherit the land. The Lord confides in those who fear him; he makes his covenant known to them. My eyes are ever on the Lord, for only he will release my feet from the snare. Turn to me and be gracious to me, for I am lonely and afflicted. Relieve the troubles of my heart and free me from my anguish.

Look on my affliction and my distress and take away all my sins. See how numerous are my enemies and how fiercely they hate me! Guard my life and rescue me; do not let me be put to shame, for I take refuge in you. May integrity and uprightness protect me, because my hope, Lord, is in you. Deliver Israel, O God, from all their troubles!

Trust, hope, wisdom, truth, mercy, love, goodness, guidance, humility, grace, refuge, and hope are all from the Lord. These are the very things that we pray for God to pour out over and through Todd, and us, in the coming days, weeks, and months. Life is sustained by and lived through the Lord who loves us more than we can understand and deeper than we can imagine.

His love and care for us beckons; it cannot be ignored or forgotten. During the valleys, we are tempted to take our eyes off of God who is ahead of us, behind us, and beside us. We are tempted to limit

His knowledge, power, and love by ultimately putting Him in a box that fits our understanding. Where are we looking to?

Today was yet again another big day in Todd's recovery. The long-awaited swallow test was finally carried out and went so well that he has no swallow restrictions and can eat all sorts of textures and consistencies of foods.

Salmon, mashed potatoes, shrimp alfredo, and fruit were just a few things on his plate for lunch and dinner today. At this point, he can eat but does not yet have much of an appetite. It will just take some time to get back into a regular diet. Since he is able to eat, he will not have to use his PEG tube. However, this will stay in for at least six weeks before it can be removed.

His therapy sessions all went quite well. The physical therapist was quite impressed with him again today and he scored a perfect score on a balance assessment.

Speech therapy for Todd involves working with his cognition and is an important part of his recovery. He will also undergo vocational rehabilitation and neurological psychology therapy.

It has been astounding to witness the hand of God move in such a manner. One of our pastors and dear friends recently described it this way: "We have marveled at the combination of a faithful, loving God; a supportive and caring community; and great medical teams throughout this journey." We simply cannot fully express our gratitude and our awe.

Our main prayer requests for tonight and tomorrow are for the Lord to prepare the way ahead for Todd. The current and future therapies are vital components in his recovery and we ask that the Lord will guide us through the decision-making process as Todd transitions to the next step. We also ask that the Lord will continue to be the Sustainer for Todd's physical, mental, emotional, and spiritual journey.

We thank you all for being such a faithful, loyal, supportive, and thoughtful support group to the Holtons. You have played a critical part in Todd's journey so far. Your time, energy, prayers, words, cards, visits, food, and help have overwhelmed us. Thank you for being involved in Todd's walk toward healing. Keep praying with us.

—Day 20 - June 19, 8:53 a.m.

Yesterday was discharge day! After doing well in his therapies and assessments this week, the rehab team decided he is ready for home.

He will have several outpatient therapy sessions in the coming weeks and months, including speech therapy, neuropsychology therapy, and vocational rehab. Although Todd is doing so well, he still has a long road of recovery ahead. These outpatient rehabs and recovery time will be crucial.

We pray that during the next few weeks and months that God's power and love will continue to sustain Todd and Faith. We pray that his enthusiasm, determination, and joy will be his continual aid and that through the struggles ahead, the voice of the Lord will be the loudest—and possibly the quietest—voice.

We appreciate the family that has formed around Todd, Faith, and our whole family. Our gratitude cannot be fully expressed. Thank you for your continued love, support, care, and prayers. Please continue to pray with us regarding the coming weeks and months for Todd, Faith, and the family. We love you all!

Psalm 57:7-11: *My heart, O God, is steadfast, my heart is steadfast; I will sing and make music. Awake, my soul! Awake, harp and lyre! I will awaken the dawn. I will praise you, Lord, among the nations; I will sing of you among the peoples. For great is your love, reaching to the heavens; your faithfulness reaches to the skies. Be exalted, O God, above the heavens; let your glory be over all the earth.*

Chapter 12
One Month Later

CaringBridge Update

Last Sunday, June 28, almost a month after Todd's heart event, he was able to stand in front of the Spring Arbor Free Methodist Church family and present a greeting of gratitude, all by the grace and power of our loving Savior and Lord.

Since the last post, Todd has transitioned home and has continued steady, speedy recovery there. He has appointments with an electrophysiologist, a cardiologist, a speech therapist, a neuropsychologist, and a general physician.

His transition home has been smooth so far, as many of you know and have witnessed first-hand. Again and again Todd expresses his overwhelming gratitude and thanks to the Lord God, whose plan is bigger than our imaginations, and to all of the family, friends, and strangers who have been critical agents of change in his life. Here we are, one month later, astounded by the goodness of God and the goodness of His Body, the Church. We are grateful for the breath of life He gives us each day.

Continue to pray with us regarding Todd's mental, emotional, spiritual, and physical health as he walks the uncertain road of recovery. May God be our focal point and our truest reason for living and breathing every day He gives.

Hebrews 11:39-40, 12:1-3: *These were all commended for their faith, yet none of them received what had been promised, since God had planned something better for us so that only together with us would they be made perfect.*

Therefore, since we are surrounded by such a great cloud of witnesses, let us throw off everything that hinders and the sin that so easily entangles. And let us run with perseverance the race marked out for us, fixing our eyes on Jesus, the pioneer and perfector of faith. For the joy set before him he endured the cross, scorning its shame, and sat down at the right hand of the throne of God. Consider him who endured such opposition from sinners, so that you will not grow weary and lose heart.

CaringBridge Update

—November 6

Todd, Faith, and their family want to thank everyone who came out to cut, split, and stack firewood, adding to the already stacked pile that was provided earlier this summer. We feel so loved, and we appreciate each of our family members, friends, neighbors, and even sweet friends from Canada who came early and stayed the whole time furnishing us with huge stacks of wood.

Later that day (October 24) we were again humbled by many who came to celebrate in the barn with us as we had a chance to say, "thank you" for loving, caring, and praying for our family these past five months.

We were excited to have two very special nurses join us in celebrating Todd's full recovery. Cheryl and Mary were exceptional and we are grateful for their extraordinary care. Thanks also to Concord Rescue's first responders Andrew, Daryl, James, Ryan, Tommy, Tom, and the Jackson County Ambulance EMTs Todd and Dan.

Farming neighbors who have helped us with wheat, bean, and corn harvest also came to our celebration—and even a very special friend, Greg Harris, from the Land Down Under!

Todd will undergo open heart surgery a week from today, on Friday, November 13, at the University of Michigan. They will repair his mitral valve with possible repair to the tricuspid valve, and close the hole in his heart. Surgery should last three to four hours, and he will be in ICU overnight. Once stable, he will be moved to a step-down and then to the post-surgical unit before being released home.

We are asking again for you to join us in prayer as we anticipate the surgery, for the medical team, successful surgery, no infection and no complications, and full recovery. We appreciate your prayers, as we have many, many times before, knowing that God

112

loves it when we come to Him humbly with our requests and the desires of our hearts.

Psalm 13:5-6: *I've thrown myself headlong into your arms—I'm celebrating your rescue. I'm singing at the top of my lungs, I'm so full of answered prayers.*

Philippians 4:6-7: *Do not be anxious about anything, but in every situation, by prayer and petition, with Thanksgiving, present your requests to God, which transcends all understanding, will guard your hearts and your minds in Christ Jesus.*

Ephesians 3:20-21: *God can do much, much more than we can ask or imagine. To Him be the glory...for all time, forever and ever.*

Chapter 13
Faith's Perspective

As we look back, we see how the threads of our lives' tapestry have been intricately selected and chosen by God; we can see that even our personalities, character traits, and experiences reveal what God allows and choses—never a wasted event or unplanned encounter. Every moment of every day is hand-picked by God. It is so evident that God's fingerprints are on our lives.

Sometimes we have to go back very far to see and sometimes we don't understand or know how God is working. One of my favorite authors, Mark Batterson, says that in this world our lives are complicated either by sins of our own commission or those of others and the evils of this world. And our lives are complicated by the blessings God brings. None of us are free of complications and challenges. It's how we view, accept, and then use those that give us the opportunity to share Christ with others, and to give God glory.

Adversity, regardless of the source, is God's tool for deepening our faith and commitment to Him. The areas in which you are experiencing the most adversity are the areas where God is at work. When we spend time reading God's Word, communing with Him, and waiting on God to reveal himself and speak to us, that is when we can allow God to calm us, clear our mind, and then fill our mind, soul, and spirit with Himself. He communes with the Holy Spirit who is present within us.

In those times when we acknowledge the Sovereign Lord and totally depend on Him in our helpless and empty state, the Holy Spirit is given full access to our lives and fills up and stretches us in ways unimaginable.

If we truly believe that, then we live freely and joyfully in the moment. We embrace and accept everything that comes into our lives knowing that God allows situations and circumstances and challenges that will bring Him glory. And the more extreme, the more difficult, the more challenging, and the more miraculous these things are, the more convincing it is that God is in control, and the more glory and praise is given to God.

The week of Todd's cardiac event we had celebrated Memorial Day at the Spring Arbor Parade and then an annual extended family picnic. About one week earlier Todd volunteered with our four-year-old grandson, Palmer to plant flowers in the Concord Cemetery urns where Todd's one set of grandparents are buried. Todd explained to Palmer that his grandparents were buried there.

Palmer in the innocence and forthright way of a youngster asked Todd when he was going to die. Todd responded with a chuckle and said, "I hope not for a while."

Later that day Palmer asked me when "T" (his nickname for Todd) is going to die. I thought it was endearing that being at the cemetery had made such a big impression on him. Several times in previous talks Palmer had been inquisitive and asked about my daddy and mommy being in heaven. So, I said, "Well, I hope it won't be for a while, but we always need to be ready, because we never know when it's our time when Jesus calls us to go home."

Then our youngest son, Thomas, came home from college for a few days before starting his summer internship, and Palmer asked, "When are you going to die, Thomas?" He followed with the question, when is T going to die?"

I had taken the whole week off from work to spend precious time with Thomas, and then I was planning on driving to Virginia by myself to attend my nephew's college graduation. At the last minute Todd, knowing I wasn't comfortable driving that far by myself, took two days off to go with me. Our middle son, Philip and his son, Palmer, live with us, but Palmer was in Ohio with his mom since we were going to be out of town for a few days.

We had a wonderful trip to Virginia. On Friday, Todd returned to work and had a full, busy day. Saturday the lumberyard is open in the morning, so afterward, since it was a rainy day with nothing urgent to do at the farm, he took up the offer to go to Cabela's with two friends for the afternoon and evening. Upon return we read a chapter in our book about communication in marriage, and then, upon Todd's request watched a movie. Our son, Philip, who was working second shift at the Jackson County Youth Center, came home and watched the last few minutes of the movie with us.

Todd and I went up to bed together shortly before midnight. After I turned out the light Todd told me of his co-worker's daughter who had rolled and totaled her car, but walked away "with but a scratch." Instantaneously he took what sounded to me like a big snore. I thought to myself, wow, I can't believe he fell immediately asleep!

His next sound no longer sounded like a snore, but a gasp, and I knew something wasn't right. I called out Todd's name at the same time turned over to turn the light on and saw that Todd was gone. His skin color was already turning an ashen gray.

I shook Todd and called out his name repetitiously. No response, no jerking, no movement whatsoever. And I thought to myself, wow, this is the way it's all going to go down, I kept thinking that to myself and I yelled down to Philip to call 9-1-1. He said, "What?" I yelled louder and more intensely, "Call 9-1-1, daddy is unresponsive."

He promptly called 911 and ran up the stairs, handed me the phone and started doing CPR. First there was no response, and then Todd's body gasped for air. I told the dispatcher, "he took a breath, now another one, no, he stopped breathing."

Philip continued with focused determination performing rhythmic CPR and calling out to his dad to "come back, Dad, take a breath, Dad, we need you, we need you, come on Dad, come on...."

He did this for what seemed like a long time. The dispatcher informed us that the ambulance was on the way, and Philip told me to go down and turn on the porch lights and be down there to show them up to the bedroom.

When the ambulance arrived, they got out their equipment and immediately relieved Philip by intubating Todd to get air into his lungs. They shocked him once, no response, waited and shocked him again, no response. On the third try his heart began beating.

As soon as the ambulance crew and first responders from Concord Rescue came, I told Philip I was going to call Todd's folks and that he should call his two brothers.

As I rode in the ambulance, I would look back at Todd and see his body shaking as he responded to the trauma of the CPR. I just kept praying out loud, calling out Jesus' name. Upon arrival at the emergency room, the ER team immediately started working on Todd, changing the temporary air flow to something more permanent.

I was asked all kinds of questions about Todd's medical history, the events of the day, and the events leading up to the cardiac arrest. The medical team put ice packs under his arms and in his groin area, a protocol they have started using for any patient dealing with heart issues of his nature. This minimizes the damage to the heart and organs and preserves the function of both. He was shaking uncontrollably.

They took him for an EKG, heart catheterization, and CAT scan of the head to see if they could come up with a diagnosis for the cardiac arrest (also called SCD—sudden cardiac death). Each test came back with no explanation other than that his Ejection Fraction (EF) was at 24%. This is a measurement of the function of the heart, and most of us have an EF of 50-65%.

Around 1:00 a.m. Philip posted on Facebook, "pray for my dad." One of my sweet cousins in Florida on vacation couldn't sleep and just felt like she should look at Facebook. She read Phil's post and cried out to the Lord, not knowing what was happening, but knowing Todd needed prayer.

My son Nathan and his wife Meg left Clare, Michigan, to come to the hospital and made it in record time. Getting the message to our other son, Thomas, was less efficient, but eventually we reached him, and before the night was over he was on his way home.

After several hours in the ER, we were told that Todd would be admitted to Intensive Care for further testing to diagnose the amount of damage to his heart and brain. We prayed with the family and friends that met, and then they left to get some sleep knowing this was going to be a long day. Further into the day family and friends started coming up to be with us, and we were overwhelmed by the care shown, just by sitting with us, giving us hugs, and shedding tears together.

Later that night with just a few close family members left, Philip, who wasn't able to stop crying, wiping his eyes and blowing his nose, came up to me and said, "Mom, I don't know why everyone is acting like Dad's going to be okay. We don't even know if he will wake up. And even if he does, what will his mental state be?"

I said, "You're right, Phil, we don't know, but look how God has already demonstrated His hand in this. Daddy and I were together and awake when I heard him take his last breath. You were home, you knew

CPR, and you were able to perform CPR until the EMTs got there. There is nothing more you could have done. You did all you could do. We now have to leave the rest up to the Lord."

On one of the days traveling with my daughter-in-law, Meg, to the hospital, I kept repeating with the confidence that comes only from the Holy Spirit speaking truth to me, "I know God can chose to heal Todd. I know he can perform a miracle. And I truly believe He is going to. I can really say, without a doubt, that God is going to heal Todd. He can do it. However, if for some reason He doesn't chose to heal him, I know that God is going to be there for us, He is going to walk with us, whatever that may look like."

When we met with the Intensivist in the ICU, he gave us the best and worst scenario that we could expect: Best case, Todd would suffer some memory loss but probably be able to function quite well and continue his past life; worst case, Todd would not wake up, or if he did, he would be in a vegetative state, needing life support or institutional care.

The uncertainty of our future could have paralyzed us with fear. Refusal to stay in that frame of mind and embracing hope that God was with us and would be with us every step gave us peace.

Throughout this journey as we sat in Todd's room together, I was so thankful for my three sons and daughter-in-law. The kids spent many hours sitting with him, fixing his pillows and covering him with blankets as his body shook from the cooling process, then putting cool washcloths on his forehead when his temperature was elevated from the infection in his body.

They talked to him, sang to him, read to him, and prayed over him. Although this has been the most difficult thing our family has experienced together, it was also a time precious to me as a mom. Experiencing my sons being so loving, caring, considerate, and true gentlemen was a comfort to witness. My kids—whose own faith was being tested and stretched.

Even though you never want your kids' hearts to be broken and their faith to waiver, I knew that they had to work out exactly what they believed regarding their view of God and how the Lord Jesus would meet them in their own separate ways.

Our neurologist met with us after his assessment of test results from an EEG and MRI of his brain. He was optimistic, yet made no promises of the degree of neurological recovery. He said there may be a day or two, or maybe even three, where we would not see any improvement. If four or five days went by without any signs of improvement, that might be the point where Todd would "stay" neurologically. It could be up to a year until we would see the full neurological status.

After that meeting, one of my prayers was to see some sign of improvement each day. I spent many hours holding Todd's hand as I sat or stood by his bed. At the beginning his hands were cold due to the arctic sun treatment that deliberately lowered his body temperature. When they brought him back up to normal temperature, the pneumonia in his lungs fevered his body, making even his hands hot. Some days his hands were so bloated from the steroids and fluids they were pumping into his body that he couldn't even close them.

Most days his hands were tied in restraints to the bed rails so he wouldn't unconsciously pull out the irritating and uncomfortable tube down his throat that provided air while allowing the medical staff to suction out the toxic gunk in his lungs.

However, each day we had encouraging news; whether it was the levels in his blood work coming closer to therapeutic range, or that his IV medications were being weaned one by one. I remember one day in particular when I didn't see any difference, and I wondered, *will this be the day that I see no improvement, will this be one day, or will it lead to day two, day three....*

Later in the evening I went back into his room and noticed his pupils for the first time since he opened his eyes. They were no longer dilated! They looked like the eyes I had looked into for many years. That to me was a sign that Todd was coming back. I said, "That's all I need, Lord. Thank You!"

There was only one day when I felt fearful. The medical staff was lowering his sedatives to evaluate his alertness and response of "purposeful movement on command," a phrase we used over and over again, and one I will never forget. As they weaned Todd off sedation, his body spontaneously became uncontrollable and agitated. I had never witnessed how a body reacts when coming off sedatives and other drugs after 10 days. It was very hard to witness, especially with my husband who very rarely demonstrated any kind of physical anger.

This was equal to—if not more—disturbing and frightening than the lifeless form I had witnessed at the start. That was the lowest point for me during this whole journey. I surely didn't want the boys to experience that.

Meg and I were in his room at the time, and this experience left both of us very discouraged. Meg was my crutch during this trial. She was a very strong young lady who accompanied me into the room whenever reports, explanations, or updates arrived from the medical team. She took notes so we could read over them and ask questions if we didn't understand anything. She later used those notes when writing the Caring Bridge daily blogs—a wonderful way to communicate with family and friends.

Meg answered texts, phone calls, and emails, and spent many, many hours communicating to Todd as if he could hear and understand every word she said. Later in his recovery she used her sign language and lip reading skills to communicate with Todd because he was unable to talk with a respirator down his throat. Communicating became frustrating, but Meg was patient and kind. I gave up more easily and would turn my head trying not to let Todd see me laugh as his sincere desire to communicate ended with no connection—which then turned into laughter from both of us.

The support of our families, friends, and acquaintances was overwhelming. We have been humbled time after time. It is unbelievable how many people have reached out to us. I am grateful for everyone who has touched our lives, and for the many prayers and cries out to God on behalf of Todd and our family. I pray often that God will bless all those who have blessed us. This is not just a "Todd miracle" or a "Holton family miracle." This is a praying global village miracle. When the people of God stormed heaven in prayer, God's heart was moved and His hand reached out and touched and healed Todd. Of this I am certain.

There are days when I know this to be true in my heart. But on many days, I have to allow the Holy Spirit to remind me of these truths and to rehearse them over again in my mind.

Here is what I know to be true: If we truly believe that God is orchestrating our lives, then we can live freely and joyfully in the moment. We can embrace and accept everything that comes into our lives, knowing that God allows situations, circumstances, and challenges that will bring Him glory. The more extreme, difficult, challenging, and miraculous the circumstance—the more evidence we have that God is in control, and the more glory and praise we can offer to God.

To God be the glory!

Chapter 14
A Blessed Family (by Faith)

Early in Todd's hospital stay I mentioned to our family that when Todd recovers, we need to have a celebration of life and thank-you party for the many people who walked with us in this journey.

Within minutes of the first responders working on and resuscitating Todd to get vital signs, Philip called his brothers and I called Todd's folks. What we wanted and needed was for our family to be with us. Having Todd's parents living nearby allows us to share a closeness that has been a huge blessing in our lives over our three decades of marriage. This was just another reminder to us how blessed our family is to have loving parents/grandparents who support us in so many ways.

Each of our siblings—five between the two of us—and their families have loved, prayed, called, cried, sat many hours in the hospital, and encouraged us. Four of our siblings live out of state, and one out of the country. They had to travel many miles to be with us and ultimately to celebrate with us.

Then there was the extended family and all the friends and neighbors who showed up right away asking what they could do. These people completed our "To Do" list: dropped off food, mowed our lawn, walked and fed our dogs, and did chores. The cards that came in the mail, food brought to the hospital, the flowers, gift cards, and gifts of money, and loads and loads of firewood, still bring me to tears as I recall how humbled and overwhelmed I felt at the tremendous demonstrations of love and support by so many.

People have shared that there were many groups of people who prayed. Our church family gathered and prayed after the morning services on May 31. Many family members and friends all over the United States and beyond lifted Todd and our family in prayer.

I believe that through this event many who know and love Christ Jesus have been encouraged and their faith renewed. I also believe some who aren't sure about it all may think about it and draw a little closer to understanding the fact that God *does* hear our prayers. His heart *is* moved by those who cry out to Him, and He *loves* to answer our prayers.

We are eternally grateful for our God who performs miracles, our friends and neighbors who have blessed us many different ways, and our family who love us, support us, and have stuck with us through it all.

A verse that comes to mind is Philippians 1:3-4: *Every time you cross my mind, I break out in exclamations of thanks to God. Each exclamation is a trigger to prayer. I find myself praying for you with a glad heart.*

Meg, Nate, Joann, Roy, Todd, Faith, Phil, Thomas, Palmer (in front)

Chapter 15

Into the Stream of History (by Todd)

I had surgery on November 13 at the University of Michigan Hospital in Ann Arbor with surgeon Dr. Steve Bolling. He took me on as a case because I had died back in May and he said, "Usually people in your state don't make it to see me."

For him it was a fairly routine surgery. It took about three hours and he basically re-pleated one of the ruptured leaflets in my mitral valve. The procedure involved stopping my heart, turning it upside down to gain access to that valve, making the repair, and installing a stainless steel partial ring sewn right into the valve itself to hold it all together.

Dr. Bolling said the surgery went just fine and observed, "You will probably live to be an old man and die of something completely different."

But this is the interesting thing: Talking with him after the operation, he explained to my wife and me that there were a lot of calcium deposits around the valve and on the heart muscle itself, which tells him that this mitral valve had been leaking for decades. I would probably have lived a normal life another 10-20 years or so, and had I survived, I would likely have needed a complete heart transplant.

So the ironic thing is this: The event that killed me last May actually saved my life—for now. As I recover at home, sitting a lot and bored to death, I am reminded of all those who have gone before me to help pave the way, and my family history comes alive.

If I had died and stayed dead, I would have become a part of the magnificent stream of Holton history. Keeping me alive into this after-life on earth gives me the privilege to not only set down my story, but also to acquaint you with a few fascinating excerpts from that story.

My sister and I were talking about how we, growing up, were very blessed with Christian influence on both our Mom's and Dad's sides of the family. We started relating to each other some of the things our grandparents told us when we were younger—even about their parents. And when you put it all together, you see yourself as a part of history, keeping it alive through stories and passing them down for future generations.

I see now how my life fits with the family lore. I stand with relatives who were veterans of the revolutionary war, one from the war of 1812, and several from the Civil War.

My son Philip's middle name is Palmer, named after the revolutionary war soldier Nathanial Palmer. One time my grandpa, Mom, and I went out to where Palmer is buried in New York. He was honored at a big dedication of a marker in the cemetery claiming his revolutionary war status.

Fast forward to the Civil War and I am reminded that Grandpa Kingsbury told me his grandfather, Francis Kingsbury, was a farmer in Deerfield, Michigan, and he didn't know if they even had a gun. But he got into the war fever and joined the 15th Michigan Infantry and within a month was taken by train down to Cairo, Illinois, put on a side-paddle-wheeler named the War Eagle, and sent down the Ohio River to the Cumberland River, then up the Cumberland to Fort Donaldson and eventually a Pittsburg landing for the battle of Shiloh, Tennessee.

On the way, the War Eagle got stuck on a sand bar and for several hours was stranded as other ships went by. Many of the soldiers on the other ships were all yelling to them, "You're gonna miss the war!" Well, a lot of those soldiers died because on the first day of the battle they were vastly outnumbered and were pretty much annihilated. So we feel it was providential that the sandbar incident saved my great great grandpa's life.

Because they were late in the afternoon getting to the battle, a general said, "Get these men right up into the line."

They were with a Wisconsin Infantry group, and when asked, "How come these men aren't firing?" their commander said, "We weren't issued any ammo when we got off the ship because you were in such a hurry...."

So they went back to the ship for ammo, and meanwhile the other infantry men on the front line were killed. If Francis Kingsbury hadn't survived the war, Grandpa Kingsbury would never have come along, and where would I be?

But Grandpa told me, even then, when they did get into battle, it rained all night while our ships were lobbing mortars into the confederacy. Due to the noise they couldn't get any sleep and were already fatigued, and tens of thousands of confederate troops—this was the second largest Civil War battle and the largest in the western campaign—were trying to push Francis and his Union compatriots into the river.

More ships kept coming in all night long reinforcing the Union side, and by the end of the next day it became a Union victory pushing the Confederates back to Corinth, Mississippi.

During that time Francis Kingsbury was found sitting shell shocked at the base of a tree—a farm boy overwhelmed by all the people, violence, noise, and death. They took him back to the Pittsburg landing where he was put on a hospital ship and taken up to St. Louis where he spent a couple months recovering from no visible wounds, then later shipped home.

When he got home, his wife knew that he loved tea and made him hot tea. Without thinking, he gulped it down and scalded the inside of his throat— still pretty much mentally out of it for a long time. Eventually he lived to lead a normal life.

Francis's daughter, Mame, got pregnant out of wedlock and the father of this child disappeared. The child born, William Kingsbury, was raised by his grandfather. He related these stories to his son Linford—the father of my mother—and my Grandpa Linford told such stories to me. In 1994, Grandpa, his son Bill (my uncle), and my son Philip and I traveled to the battlefields of Tennessee to see Fort Donaldson and Shiloh where Francis fought.

So I'm part of this amazing history, and it seems fitting to add my story to the ongoing narrative.

My grandma June Crots, wife of Grandpa Linford, tells the story of her great grandfather Lewis Ostrander who was with the 14th Ohio Volunteer Infantry and was captured during the Civil War at the Battle of Chickamauga, Georgia. He was taken prisoner for 16 months and ended up in the notorious Andersonville, Georgia, prison. I visited the prison—what a place!—where he claimed to have survived by eating a potato a day. By the end of the war he had lost all of his teeth.

His wife, Alzada, wrote a letter "To whom it may concern." I don't have the actual letter to quote, but basically she said, "My husband has been taken prisoner, and last I knew he was at Andersonville, GA. Could you please inform me whether he is living or dead? Send this message to Alzada Ostrander, Sylvania, Ohio."

They already had four kids, he was older when he went to war, and she died shortly after he left. So he came back from Georgia and married Abigail Hosner. A common motive for younger women marrying these veterans was for their pensions. Also, men were scarce This new couple had three more kids. He's an old man with a long beard in the picture I have, and he's holding a young daughter.

June Crots Kingsbury also told me that her father died in 1929 at the beginning of the Great Depression when she was only 12. Her mother, Nellie, raised seven kids and a step-son by herself on 40 acres during the Depression, and they all came out well. They were right next door to a little Wesleyan Church, and attending that church molded those kids in a positive way.

The other interesting family story—as I thought back on the Christian influence I got from my ancestors—is this: My ancestor Emma Palmer married Frank Smith and they were charter members of the Prairie Free Methodist Church north of Deerfield, Michigan. Grandpa Kingsbury, whom I saw in Heaven, said that one Christmas when he was a kid, his dad (William, whose wife Ida played the pump organ) loaded the pump organ onto a wagon and took it to the church for the Christmas pageant.

At that time this church allowed no musical instruments in the building, and after getting it all set up, the pastor came in and asked them to remove it from the church. So grandpa loaded the organ back onto the wagon, pulled it around to the side of the church up toward a window by the front. They opened the window and Ida played the organ where it could be heard inside the church for the pageant.

Now, on my dad's mother's side of the family there was an Ebenezer Shoff who had a farm in South Boliver in western New York. A fella came along one day and said he'd really like to buy that farm. Every time he came around, this man increased the offer until—in the 1870s—Ebenezer accepted what seemed like a lot of money for the farm and left to run a hotel near Angelica, NY.

This man quietly bought up quite a few farms and shortly thereafter began drilling for oil. One of the first ones was the Shoff well, and the story has it Ebenezer was so mad he was going to take a gun to court with him, but legally there was nothing he could do because he had signed off on the farm. He felt so completely upset and detached from that whole area that he pulled up stakes and the whole family moved west and took up free government land in South Dakota where his son, Seymour, and daughter-in-law both became pastors at the Sedgwick Free Methodist Church.

Another son, Alonson, met Hilda Johnson who at 16 came from Sweden. They married and settled in the same area. They were the grandparents of my father. After several years of the hardships on the prairie with fires, droughts, Indian scares, and hard winters, they sold out and moved to Illinois where Hilda's real estate developer brother sold them a farm that turned out to be a bad deal. In the early 1920s they lost the farm and moved to Bangor, Michigan, where Hilda and Alonson's children Vernon, Erwin, Nathalie, Myrtle, and Ray started their Michigan adventure.

At that time Alonson felt he was losing his children. His oldest son quit going to church and was into automobiles. The second son had an alcohol problem and was drifting away. The younger three he dropped off at church one day and took the horse and buggy back home, and when he got home the son Erwin showed up. The father asked where he'd been, and Erwin said he was helping a neighbor fix a roof and had decided to spend the night. He came home that Sunday morning with alcohol on his breath. Alonson said, "Would you be proud of your mother seeing you like this?"

The son replied, "You mean like you—not going to church—you hypocrite?"

This shook Alonson to his core. He had drifted away from the Lord, and he went into the bedroom, fell on his knees, and started to pray. He felt like he lost his two older sons. The younger two girls liked flapper music and wanted to put their hair up, so he felt he was losing them. He looked up from the bed into the dresser mirror and saw the face of Jesus speaking right to him, that he needed to be the spiritual leader of the house so the Lord could bless him and his family.

He turned around, climbed back into the buggy, and went back to church. He slipped in the back door of the church where Pastor Cryderman was preaching. After the service Pastor Cryderman shook his hand, and Alonson said, "I will never miss church again."

Alonson did become the spiritual leader of his home and sent his two daughters to Spring Arbor for their education. That's where Nathalie met and married Don McDonald, and my Grandma Myrtle met and married Elwood Holton. Elwood became the Sunday school superintendent of the Benton Harbor Free Methodist Church, and in the spring of 1943 after a bad flood, told my dad to take his socks and shoes off, roll up his pants, and walk up to the church.

He would be there shortly. Elwood had to go to the neighbors to plug in their basement sump pump. They later found him electrocuted, face down in the water.

This left Myrtle with two young boys—a my dad who was eight years old, and his younger brother Gordon. In 1947 they moved to Spring Arbor where she worked at the Post Office and boarded students.

Thus, my dad didn't have a father for most of his growing up years, but he did have good mentors. One was his Uncle Don "Mac" McDonald, and another was Bill Houghtby who owned the lumber and coal company which my dad bought in 1960.

I didn't have a grandpa on that side of the family, but I do have memories of Great Grandfather Frank Holton (my dad's grandpa). He was the sexton of the Spring Arbor Cemetery. My sister and I helped him place flags on the veterans' graves before Memorial Day. In the fall of 1975 I traveled with him, my great aunt, and my dad to the Upper Peninsula where the Holtons were from.

As we traveled, Grandpa Frank told us of how the Holtons came to the United States from Canada in the early 1880s. Frank's father Nathaniel married Catherine Trickey Jones, who was widowed and already had a son named Billy. These three along with several families from Owen Sound, Ontario, placed all their belongings onto barges, and a single tugboat towed these barges north along the east shore of Lake Huron. This route took them up to Sault St. Marie and down the St. Mary's river to a place in Michigan called the Barbau Settlement about 14 miles south of the Soo Locks.

The Upper Peninsula of Michigan was wild and untamed. Nathanial bought 120 acres about a mile east of the St. Mary's River—what is now 14 ½ mile road. Thereafter he erected a crude log structure for the winter of 1882, spent the next year cutting large white pine trees, and by the next fall had built a nice 18' by 22' story-and-a-half log home.

Frank was born there on November 22, 1883. He would be one of 14 children to be raised there. The winters were long, the rocks and stumps plentiful. True pioneers, the family joined the Hay Lake Free Methodist Church. Later, by using horses, Frank helped move that building three miles north on the River Road to the town of McCarron.

In the early 1900s, Frank witnessed another impressive event when the Army Corp of Engineers dug the Neebish Cut, a place between the mainland and Michigan's Neebish Island where the channel was too narrow and shallow for big ships. They blasted and hauled rocks to make the channel wide and deep enough that southbound ships could pass Neebish Island without waiting.

Frank and Margaret Holton at Neebish Cut

This Neebish Cut set the stage for large Great Lakes ships, which brings me to our November evening in 1975. As we stood right on the shore at Martin Welsh's place where the St. Mary's is almost as narrow as it can get, Martin said to the four of us, "You're about to see the second-largest Great Lakes freighter come through."

So we waited. The sun was starting to set, but it was still light enough. Pretty soon, sure enough, along comes this great behemoth of a ship sitting high in the water because it was empty. It was lit up like a Christmas tree. We could view the longshoreman walking along the rails of the ship. They looked at us, and we looked at them. They seemed so close I felt like I could almost reach out and touch them.

As I relate this story, it's been 40 years, but I can still feel and hear the rumble and hum of the engines of the Edmond Fitzgerald as it passed us by on its last journey north.

*   *   *   *   *

Grandpa Frank wanted to see the old place where he was born, and also the place up the road where he had farmed and built a big barn. He used to milk cows and deliver milk to town with a 1929 Ford delivery panel truck identified on the side as "Holton Dairy."

As we wandered around inside the old log house, you could see the perfectly fitted joints of the Michigan white pine logs still in great shape. Grandpa Frank told us he was born upstairs, first room on the right. He said how his dad, Nathanial, was a fairly hard man who expected a

Frank's son Elwood Holton

lot from his children, work-wise. They picked stones from fields until their hands bled, and worked at blowing stumps with dynamite and clearing the land for farming. He also kept the peace with a razor strap if needed, and he would let those children not doing their part know it.

Sixteen years later in 1991, Bob and Hazel Burbo gave me the house. We took it apart log by log, board by board, and moved it to our Concord, Michigan, farm where it has since been completely restored including a new cedar shake roof.

During the dismantling of this log house, in taking apart the stairway that went into the basement, I found a razor strap around the backside of an upright post. I asked Bob, who had lived in the house until 1966, if this was his. He said, "I have never seen that before in my life and I bought this house in the 1940s."

The strap is about three inches wide, maybe 18 inches long, and has a metal clip at the top end so you could hang it in your barber shop, and at the bottom is a piece of leather sewn to it—leather on one side and a canvas material on the other side. It was originally used in a barber shop for sharpening a straight razor, but Frank's dad used it for disciplinary purposes. It now hangs on a wall of my house as a reminder of the "good old" days.

Log house on location at left, moved and restored on right.

As Great Grandfather would say, "Those weren't the good old days. You're living in the good old days."

Grandpa Frank talked about losing a brother at childbirth, and his dad burying the baby out back under an apple tree. He also told us about his grandmother, Margaret Barber Reid, who came from Ireland with her parents to Canada in the 1840s. She married Thomas Holton, also from Ireland, but he died after both of his sons were born.

Margaret then married John Reid. They had several children including a son also named John Reid, half-brother to Frank's dad Nathanial. John married Jane Trickey, sister to Frank's mother Catherine Trickey, so two sisters married two half-brothers.

Each of these families had children. One was my Great Grandfather Frank, and one was Margaret Reid, Frank's double first cousin. They were great friends and were married in 1905. This fact didn't come out in the family stories for a very long time because one of Frank's daughters, Margaret, who was a missionary to Africa from 1938 to 1962, told me when I was small, "We live in the present, not in the past—you don't need to know about all those things from the past...."

Margaret left for Africa in 1938 under the Free Methodist Church Mission Board for a five year stint. During that time she lost her mother, her brother, and a sister. Her father Frank remarried Martha Izzard, widow of George Izzard, a rival of Frank's. The two of them had the two best teams of pulling horses in all the eastern Upper Peninsula, and they always competed with each other at horse pulls.

It was common knowledge that George was not a very nice man. After he died in the mid-1940s, Frank married Martha and treated her with love and respect until she died early in 1975. Grandpa talked about taking his large team of Percherons to the "Soo," then by train west to Tahquamenon Falls to earn extra money hauling logs in the winter.

This trip was Frank's last journey to the north. On November 10, 1975, the Edmond Fitzgerald sank in rough Lake Superior waters just 15 miles from Whitefish Bay where Frank subsequently had two small summer cabins and where my dad and Uncle Gordon spent a lot of time. Grandpa was awestruck at how such a large ship could simply disappear.

Grandpa entered Mercy hospital in Jackson, his body failing, a large, tall man with huge hands. On November 22, 1975, we sang "Happy Birthday" to celebrate his 92 years. With tears streaming down his cheeks, his final words to many of us were, "I want to see all of you in heaven some day." On December 2, he went to meet Jesus personally.

I can hear Jesus say to Frank, "Well done, good and faithful servant." And I live for the day when Jesus says those same words to me and I can see all those folks who helped prepare the way for me.

"This world is not my home," says one of the old gospel songs I love, "I'm just a' passing through. My treasures are laid up somewhere beyond the blue. The angels beckon me from heaven's open door, and I can't feel at home in this world anymore." Kevin Ganton and I sang this song on a Sunday evening church service before Pastor Darold Hill preached.

Chapter 16
Return to Haiti

A few people may have thought I was crazy, but by February of 2016 I was ready for another trip to Haiti. I felt compelled to thank Pastor—now Bishop—Devariste Elidor and the Park Christian Church for their timely prayers that truly helped heal my body at a crucial time. As I recounted earlier, two or three thousand of these Haitians had prayed for me at 10:00 a.m. on a Friday right during the time when I was returning to consciousness and the doctor said, "Whatever he is like when he wakes up—this is the way he will probably be for the rest of his life."

So with high expectations on Sunday, February 15, I headed for Port-au-Prince, Haiti, along with 11 others from our church group. I was on the right hand side of the plane as we came into Haiti, and an overwhelming sense of love and warmth and gratitude came over me for just being able to return. The plane landed followed by the usual hassles at customs and getting our luggage out of the airport onto trucks felt very familiar.

Seeing my driver, John Wiliar, was special. He was as glad to see me as I was to see him. My wife and I have sponsored his daughter through the Free Methodist International Childcare Ministries at $25 a month since 2001, and now she is a senior in high school. So John and I gave each other a look of "very glad to see you" and a long embrace.

The purpose of this trip was for our team to help establish secure boundaries for a new property purchased to function as the Friends of Haiti Organization (FOHO) headquarters. Their previous building was destroyed in the January 10, 2010 earthquake. This project entailed digging into the ground to establish rock foundations for the whole perimeter wall, and building a generator house, a house for the caretaker, and a gathering place pavilion.

In the future this property will hold the International Childcare Ministry center, FOHO guest house and orientation site for visiting teams, and a shop for all our equipment, tools and trucks. Eventually the superintendent hopes to have a church on that property. This three-acre site is situated beside a river across from banana and sugar cane farms. The view is spectacular. You can see the mountains in several directions.

It's hot, dry, and dusty, and looks barren now, but we anticipate that within a couple years, working through the Eden Tree Reforestation program, to plant several species of native trees for shade and crops—bananas, coconut, mango, and so on.

We worked there, but we stayed at a place called Vi Vi Michelle, up a little higher on the side of the mountain in an area of nice homes. The Free Methodist Church has a mission house there. From our vantage point we could watch the sun rise each morning over the eastern mountains of the Dominican Republic at 6:10 a.m. Sunrise was the highlight of my day. We could also look down the valley and actually see our worksite two or three miles away.

The team worked well together. I had the privilege of taking two of my nephews , Peter Moyer (whose parents are missionaries in France), and Graham Colton from Lancaster Country, Pennsylvania. Both these fellas knew French, so we used them occasionally for translation, and we also hired a Haitian young man named Gary as an interpreter. At one point during the week we had as many as 45 Haitians working with us doing the cement work, digging, and block-laying. This gave them an opportunity to make some wages for those 10 days.

On February 25 it was my great privilege to be invited to speak at the Park Christian Church in the morning service which started at 6:00 a.m. and ran until about 10:30 a.m. After a break, they had Sunday school from 11:00 a.m. until 12:30 p.m.

I was asked by Bishop Devariste to address the congregation of about 2,000, and give them a short version of my story. It was a very emotional experience for me to realize that many of the folks in this congregation had prayed for me at that crucial time. Now I was on the very spot of those prayers. I had my nephew Peter interpret for me. He did a great job, although a few words were hard to put into the Creole dialect of French they speak in Haiti.

I was able to relate the stories of my passing, what I had seen, heard, and envisioned during those moments. I held my Bible up and challenged the people: "Do you believe this is the true word of God?" They said "yes," and I said, "Do you believe this book can change your life?" They said "yes," and I said, "Do you believe this book can save you?" Of course, they always said "yes." Then I briefly shared what God has done for me and how their prayers surely made a difference.

Bishop Devariste was sick in bed the Sunday I was there so he couldn't attend the service. He's a very commanding man, over six feet tall, and when I visited him in his office on Friday, he stood up from behind his desk, came around to give me a big hug, and said, "I'm really glad to see you."

We talked a little of the struggles Haiti has and the church responsibilities that now rest on him. But he said, "With God's help, all is possible."

After church and greeting the many people I have known for several years, the team went to a local restaurant for lunch, then back to our house to reflect on the thoughts of the day. It was exhausting and emotionally challenging, but I felt I had to do it and that God was in it. God blessed not only me, but also those who heard through interpretation what God had to say through me.

The rest of my time in Haiti was predictable, with routine work schedules and I felt very good. The last couple days it was in the 90s and I could feel my body starting to overheat, so we made sure we always had water to drink and shade to sit under. But I really felt physically that God had healed me to the point where I could do what I would have been able to do if none of the events of the past year had happened at all. I picked up cement blocks, moved rocks, tolerated the heat, and did a lot of driving— probably the most I've ever done in Haiti. I drove to get supplies and to take people back and forth to the old mission house where Pastor Dottie was teaching at the Bible school and where we were working on a vehicle. That trip averaged about an hour one way, and it gave me a lot better idea of how to strike out and go anywhere in Haiti.

We did have one day off on Saturday. We hired a team to take us north and west along the ocean to Wahoo Bay. This place has a beautiful hotel overlooking the Caribbean with its turquoise blue water. Six of us piled into a little wooden boat and two Haitians motored us a quarter mile or so down the beach to some reefs where, for $7 each, we could take the boat ride and rent a mask, fins, and snorkel. We paddled around there on the reef for a good half hour. It struck me as rather odd that this beautiful place was just across the street from where people lived in poverty and dinky tin shacks.

After the relaxing day by the ocean we returned to Port-au-Prince before dark—it's very important to get in before dark because of the multiple dangers in this country. It starts getting dark by 4:30 p.m. and is pretty well dark by 6:00 p.m.

Every time I leave Haiti I get this sense of longing to go back. As the plane took off, I could look out my window and see our job site from up in the sky. From that distance it looked small, but the small things we can do are worthwhile. Little is much when God is in it. That's the way I always feel when I leave Haiti.

So now, going from 90 degree weather in Haiti to snow in Michigan, I'm reminded of God's love, His grace, and His ultimate plan for the future—whatever that may be and however it may involve my life. For my part, I'll try to be a good husband, a good dad, a good granddad, a good employee, a good employer, and daily I look to see what God has in store for me. Each day is a new day. May God be praised. To God be the glory.

Acknowledgments

I have *everybody* to thank and will attempt to list a whole bunch of them here:

- My wife, Faith, our three boys Nathan, Philip, and Thomas and their families, my brother Kyle and Jeanne and their family, and my sister JoLynne and Jim and their family.

- Meg Holton, my daughter-in-law, who was prompted and guided by the Holy Spirit as she documented my story on *CaringBridge.*

- My father and mother who consistently show God's love and the value of prayer and hard work.

- Pastors Mark and Linda Van Valin and Darold and Marg Hill.

- Cheryl and Mary, extraordinary nurses in the ICU at Allegiance Hospital, and Darlene Granger and Connie Fenton who monitored my progress and assisting in daily injections.

- Spring Arbor Free Methodist Church family.

- Spring Arbor Lumber Company and employees.

- The many groups I am involved with including Sons of Union Veterans of the Civil War, 1st Michigan Light Artillery 3rd Battery, and Concord and Spring Arbor area farmers including Brent Hotchkin, Arthur and Bruce Riske, Jeff Ropp, Bob Clark, Marv DeVisser, and Jim Hubbard.
- Cascades chapter of the Veteran Motor Car Club of America and old car friends who helped me on my restorations: Stan Lyon, Leo Warren, Ken Soderbeck, Dean Nelson, Jamie Kulawik, Mary Jo Hesselback, and John Neagley.
- Tyler and Leah White, animal feeders.
- Scott and Jennifer Pelham, Phantom Lawn Mowers.
- Classmates Scott Pelham and Kevin Sanford for organizing friends who delivered and stacked many loads of firewood.
- Hesston College, Hesston, Kansas, and my Mennonite friends and all those whom God has placed in my path along life's journey.
- Dan Runyon who interviewed me, took down my stories, put this book together, and published it as part of a class project for Spring Arbor University copy editing students who made

many improvements: Hannah Blume, Nathaniel Bortz, Madeline Hooker, Brianna Loomis, Alexa Matthews, and Simon Reidsma. Anne Paine-Root and others did final proofing.

I agreed to write my story if it would be an encouragement to others, and I would like to close with my favorite Bible verse:

Love must be sincere. Hate what is evil; cling to what is good. Be devoted to one another in love. Honor one another above yourselves. Never be lacking in zeal, but keep your spiritual fervor, serving the Lord. Be joyful in hope, patient in affliction, faithful in prayer. Share with the Lord's people who are in need. Practice hospitality.

—Romans 12:9-13

—To God be the glory—

CPSIA information can be obtained
at www.ICGtesting.com
Printed in the USA
LVOW04s1623090516
487382LV00015B/728/P